Financial
Stewardship

by

Andrew Wommack

Harrison House

14 13 12   10 9 8 7 6 5 4 3 2 1

Financial Stewardship

ISBN: 978-160683-400-8
Copyright © 2012 by Andrew Wommack Ministries, Inc.
PO Box 3333
Colorado Springs, CO 80934-3333

Published by Harrison House Publishers
PO Box 310
Shippensburg, PA 17257
www.harrisonhouse.com

Table of Contents

Preface

I remember giving my tithes faithfully to the Lord as a young child. I don't think I have ever received a dollar that I didn't give a tithe from it. I was blessed to a degree, but the traditions and doctrines of men made financial prosperity come hard for me (Mark 7:13).

I was married with two children and had been in ministry for over twenty-five years before I really began to get the revelation of the things I'm sharing with you in this book. And I'm telling you, it has made a huge difference. It has not only made a big difference in my life personally, but I could not be fulfilling God's instructions to me without the financial abundance these truths have produced in our ministry.

At one time, I loved God with all my heart and was serving Him to the best of my ability and understanding, yet I was so strapped financially that I couldn't fulfill the instructions He was giving me. I've struggled more in this area than in any other area of my Christian life.

And I'm not alone in this. I remember being a part of a group of ministers who went to Oral Roberts'[1] home in 2009 to visit

---

[1]One of the most well-known Christian leaders and healing evangelists of the twentieth century. He pioneered television evangelism, laid groundwork of prosperity and abundant life teachings, and founded Oral Roberts University in Tulsa, Oklahoma.

with him just a year before he died. He ministered to all of us and then he let each one of us ask him a question. One minister asked, "What is the hardest thing you have ever endured in your ministry?"

I was intrigued by that question. Here was a man who had a person shoot a gun at him at point-blank range and the bullet missed. He has been persecuted as few ministers of our day have. He has dealt with scandals of his own and in his family, which eventually cost him the university that he founded. I was eager to hear his response.

He didn't hesitate one moment. He said, "The hardest thing I've ever endured was financial problems." He spoke of many sleepless nights spent in agony over finances. He spoke of being pressed at every turn in his ministry by the restraints lack of money had placed upon him. I could relate as I'm sure you can.

There was a time in my life that it didn't matter how excited I was about the directions the Lord was giving me. Regardless of the enthusiasm or opportunity, my one dominant thought was, *How can I afford to do this?* Thank God, that is no longer an issue.

I'm not saying that I have an unlimited supply of money. I am saying that I have come to a place in my faith that I know I can always get the finances needed to accomplish God's instructions. I am no longer limited by money. That is liberating.

These truths the Lord has shown me can work for anyone—including you. I pray that as you read this book, the Holy Spirit will enlighten you in a way that only He can. If you have been struggling financially as I once was, I believe a spirit of poverty will be broken off of you and you will come into a new place where the only factor that limits you is God's will, not whether or not you have the money to do it!

Introduction

The Sunday comics and money are both printed on paper, but one makes people laugh and the other makes them cry. The actual paper that money is printed on is pretty much worthless—not much different from the stuff used to manufacture Kleenex. In reality, money only has value because people agree to view it as valuable. The dollar, the euro, and the yen are nothing more than creations of men used to trade for services, but arguing about the real value of money isn't going to put food on the table. The world's system of trade is based on money, and we all have to use it to survive.

The influence of money in our lives is very real, so it isn't surprising that Jesus taught more on the subject of finances than on any other single topic. He taught more about managing resources than He did on prayer or even faith—which tells us that the topic of money, and how we handle it, is very important. One of the reasons the church hasn't made more of an impact on modern society seems obvious to me: we haven't successfully applied the Gospel to everyday concerns. Most people are so occupied with trying to deal with earthly problems that they aren't thinking about the eternal. But the Gospel has a lot to say about everyday earthly concerns—especially finances.

I know money is a sore subject that a lot of people want to avoid, but learning how God views finances is basic Christianity. Jesus said that if you can't be faithful in your finances, then you can't be trusted with anything (Luke 16:11 *NIV*)! Not surprisingly, what the Bible has to say about financial stewardship is different from most of what you will hear from business sources that teach on "asset management." God doesn't operate by this world's system, and it's more important for us to understand how God's financial system works than it is to understand Wall Street.

Some people have a tendency to get offended when ministers start talking about money—especially when that minister is on television. The truth is, we have all been given plenty of reason to get offended. A lot of people have been taken advantage of in this area.

Recently, I was appalled by what I saw going on during a fundraiser on a Christian television network. It was pure manipulation and hype. It was totally wrong. I'm not saying this to criticize other ministers, but we have to acknowledge that, in some cases, manipulation and hype are out there—especially concerning finances. What really bothers me is that those carnal techniques work!

Many in the body of Christ are so uninformed in the area of finances that people fall for manipulation tactics all the time. For example, some evangelist or minister on TV says, "Send me $1,000 and your prayers will be answered," and people send money by the truckload. But the kingdom of God doesn't operate that way; you can't buy God's favor.

Introduction

So, yes, there are abuses in the body of Christ regarding money, but don't miss out on benefitting from the truths in God's Word about finances just because a few people are abusing the topic. I encourage you to set aside right now any past upsets or offenses you might have suffered, and allow the Word of God to reveal finances to you from a godly perspective. I believe that you'll be glad you did.

In this book, I won't be outlining the steps involved in forming a budget, or the nuts and bolts of managing your income. Other resources for that kind of practical wisdom are already available. I'm going to be teaching the Scriptural principles that go to the heart of financial problems—and success. By fixing your heart, you deal with the root cause of financial situations, and then money will take care of itself. Once your heart is right, using wisdom in how you spend your money comes naturally.

We can't fall into the trap of compartmentalizing our lives into the spiritual realm where we relate to God, and everyday life where we deal with jobs, family, finances, and everything else. A house divided will not stand for long (Matthew 12:25), and confining our interaction with God to a couple of hours on Sunday isn't going to produce the fruit we desire in life. Our relationship with God needs to permeate every area of our lives: marriage, business, relationships, recreation, and finances.

Finances are important, and you'll be amazed how letting God into your finances can bring peace and healing to other areas of your life—because how you view money affects a lot more than just your bank balance. My goal in this teaching is to help you discover how to turn your finances over to God and to step into true prosperity in every area of your life.

Chapter 1

Being a Steward

I teach on financial stewardship at Charis Bible College in Colorado. Almost all of the students move from out of state to attend Charis. A lot of them leave behind careers and the security of good-paying jobs. They also have to pay the cost of tuition, and being in school for several hours a day means that most of them have to take part-time jobs or get shift work. So the average student coming to school faces a decrease in salary, an increase in the cost of living, additional tuition costs, and part-time work to make ends meet. In the natural sense, it's a recipe for disaster.

Without God's intervention, those students would be in big trouble. But at the end of every year, I ask the students how many of them are better off financially than they were when they came, and at least 80 percent always say they are better off. The reason they are able to prosper in spite of natural obstacles is that at Charis, they have received a revelation on the Scriptural truths related to finances.

This doesn't work only for Bible college students. Anyone who applies the Scriptural principles I'm going to talk about can see financial prosperity begin to work in their lives—and I don't mean just an increase in wealth. You can have a totally different attitude toward money. Instead of being dominated and controlled by money, you can begin to see that money is your servant. Money can become a tool you use in life, instead of a master that rules over you. Too many Christians are slaves to money. They work at jobs they don't like and do things they don't want to do just to make ends meet. God has a better way for us to live.

Not long ago, I was in Hong Kong teaching on grace. The people were really receiving what I was teaching, but I felt a nudging in my heart to teach on the subject of finances. I was a little hesitant to follow the Holy Spirit's leading though because of the reputation American ministers have when it comes to teaching about money. I knew there could be some prejudice against me, so even though I really felt a quickening in my heart to teach on finances, I didn't do it right away.

Money is meant to be your servant, not a master that rules over you.

The conference went on for a few more days, and then the pastor of the church I was at took me out to lunch. Several of his leaders came with us and while we were waiting for the food to arrive, they started asking me questions. Nearly every question they asked was about finances. They wanted to know how to reconcile teaching on prosperity with God's grace. Giving is often presented as something you do in order to make God bless you, and they wanted to know how finances fit into the true Gospel message: God blesses us because Christ made us righteous, not because of our performance.

After visiting with the pastor and his people, I knew for sure that God had been leading me to teach on finances. So during the conference the next day, I decided to change the focus of my preaching. As I stood in front of the people, I asked, "What is the one thing you do not want to hear an American pastor preach about?"

People immediately began to shout, "prosperity," "finances," "giving and receiving."

"Well, that is exactly what God has led me to teach on," I said.

The room went completely silent; you could've heard a pin drop. I pressed on anyway and taught prosperity from a grace perspective. In the end, they loved it. As a matter of fact, the pastor emailed me after the conference to say that his staff was still getting responses. It helped his people tremendously, which shows that sometimes the things you least want to hear about will help you the most. You may feel about a financial message just like those people did initially, but I believe that this book will help you to better understand finances in the same way this teaching helped them.

The very first thing we need to understand about finances is that we are stewards of what God has given us. Jesus taught on stewardship in the parable in which He told about the shrewd manager.

In Luke 16:1, Jesus told His disciples, "There was a certain rich man, which had a steward; and the same was accused unto him that he had wasted his goods." This is an important parable that I will teach on in depth later, but for now, I just want to point out the function and attitude of being a steward. A *steward* is a person who manages someone else's property, finances, or other affairs. As Christians, we are stewards, and we need to recognize that the money we have is not really ours; it's a gift from God.

Now, you may be thinking, *I can guarantee you God didn't give me the money I have! I've worked hard for it. I've earned it.* Maybe you work two jobs, or you have scrimped for years to get a little savings, and so the money you have accumulated seems like the result of your own efforts. I understand that way of thinking, but, in reality, it isn't true.

Every good and perfect gift comes from God (James 1:17). Ultimately, God is the source of everything you have. First of all, God gave you life. You didn't cause yourself to exist—you were created. God made you and He is the source of every good thing in your life (Genesis 1:26; James 1:17).

The apostle Paul wrote, "In him we live, and move, and have our being"(Acts 17:28). God not only gave you physical life, but He is the source of your wisdom and abilities. He gave you the talents you use to earn a living. God is also the reason you were born at this time in history—the most prosperous period ever. So even though you are working hard at your job, God is still the source of your financial success. Without the blessing of God upon your life, you wouldn't even have the *ability* to prosper.

You may be out in the world actually doing the work you get paid for, but you need to develop the mindset that the money you receive doesn't belong to you; it belongs to God. Remember, God gave you your talents and abilities, and every good thing you have is a blessing from Him. God has entrusted you with all of your finances, and it is important to develop the mindset of being a steward—over God's money, not yours.

Most people see making a living as resulting from the sweat of their brow, and they don't see God as their source. They separate their lives into spiritual matters like heaven and hell, and private, personal matters like career and finances. When it comes to money, they think it's all up to them. As a result, many Christians are struggling financially. God wants to be the source of everything in your life. The Lord never intended you to carry the burden of financial responsibility, and He wants to lift that burden from you.

A lot of Christians say they know God is the source of everything, but their lives don't reflect an understanding of that truth. I was in a meeting one time when the man receiving the offering told everyone to reach into the back pocket or the purse of the person in front of them and "give like you've always wanted to give." Of course, no one actually did it. The point he was making is that we are much more likely to be generous with someone else's money. You would probably take more money from your neighbor's wallet to put in the offering than you would from your own.

When you think that money comes by your own sweat and tears, then you keep a much tighter hold on it. You become attached to your money, and it actually becomes your master. But when you see yourself as a steward and recognize money as God's blessing—even though you work for your paychecks—it totally changes the role money plays in your life. It ceases to control you and simply becomes a tool. This simple change in mindset from owner to steward will make a tremendous difference for you.

Many Christians have made a firm commitment of their lives to the Lord concerning spiritual things, but when it comes to finances, they see money as a private possession. The pressures of life lead them to view money as something they must control, and that kind of ownership mentality leads to a lot of problems.

The first step toward becoming responsible with your finances is to get this mindset that money does not belong to you. Instead of clinging to your money, you need to think: *I am a steward of what God has entrusted to me. God has blessed me with these talents and abilities. God has blessed me with my job. God has put me into a prosperous nation at the most prosperous time in all of history. God is blessing me, and God has given me all of the resources I have. It is not up to me to run my finances the way I want to. I'm a steward.*

People with an ownership mentality end up trying to do everything themselves, but stewards freely receive God's blessing. Look at how blessed Abraham was.

> *Now the LORD had said unto Abram, Get thee out of thy country, and from thy kindred, and from thy father's house, unto a land that I will shew thee: And I will make of thee a great nation, and I will bless thee, and make thy name great; and thou shalt be a blessing: And I will bless them that bless thee, and curse him that curseth thee: and in thee shall all families of the earth be blessed.*

> *Genesis 12:1–3*

God said here that *He* would bless Abraham, and that *He* would make Abraham's name great. When you read the entire story of

Abraham, you see that God wasn't talking about intangible spiritual benefits. He was talking about physical earthly blessings. Abraham didn't become rich through his own hard work. He became wealthy because the blessing of God was on his life (Hebrews 6:13–14). Abraham was blessed in everything he did. Even when he made mistakes, God blessed him.

During a famine in Canaan, Abraham traveled down into Egypt with his wife, Sarah. She was sixty-something years old at the time, but she was so beautiful that Abraham was afraid Pharaoh would kill him in order to take her from him. So Abraham lied and told Pharaoh that Sarah was his sister and not his wife! It was absolutely the wrong thing to do, and he put his wife in a terrible situation. Abraham was willing to sacrifice Sarah just to save his own neck. God had to intervene by sending plagues upon Pharaoh's house in order to get Sarah restored to Abraham (Genesis 12).

> *The blessing of God is not dependent on your performance, or according to what you deserve.*

Not even thirty years later, Abraham did the exact same thing again! He told Abimelech, king of Gerar, that Sarah was his sister. This time, God came to Abimelech in a dream and told him to restore Sarah or he would die. When Abimelech saw that God was with Abraham, he returned Sarah and gave Abraham gold, silver, cattle, sheep, and servants. Then he told Abraham that he could live anywhere in the kingdom he desired. Abraham was in the wrong in both situations, but the blessing of God never stopped causing Abraham to prosper (Genesis 20).

Abraham was not wealthy because of his shrewd business sense or because God rewarded his great integrity. Abraham was prosperous because God promised to bless him and make his name great. The blessing was independent of Abraham's performance or what he deserved. It was purely the favor of God that made him rich. In the same way, your efforts are not the source of prosperity in your life.

The blessing of God made Abraham so rich that he and his nephew, Lot, couldn't dwell together because their flocks and herds were too big. They had so many animals that one location couldn't feed them all, so their servants began fighting with one another over the grazing land, and they were forced to separate. Abraham's conversation with Lot about this situation is revealing.

> *Abram said unto Lot, Let there be no strife, I pray thee, between me and thee, and between my herdmen and thy herdmen; for we be brethren. Is not the whole land before thee? separate thyself, I pray thee, from me: if thou wilt take the left hand, then I will go to the right; or if thou depart to the right hand, then I will go to the left. And Lot lifted up his eyes, and beheld all the plain of Jordan, that it was well watered every where… Then Lot chose him all the plain of Jordan; and Lot journeyed east: and they separated themselves the one from the other.*
>
> *Genesis 13:8–11*

Abraham took Lot up to a hilltop so they could look out over the whole land. One part of the land was a well-watered plain plush with grass; the other part was dry. Keep in mind that the survival of their herds depended on there being plenty of natural grass to graze on. They couldn't go to a feed store and buy food for their flocks and cattle. Fields of grass were the only source of food they had. So it isn't surprising that Lot chose the well-watered land for himself.

This story reveals how confident Abraham was in God as his source. Anyone who was relying on natural circumstances and his own efforts for prosperity would never give up a well-watered plain for his animals. Looking at the natural facts, the decision of whether to choose a grassy plain or the desert was a no-brainer. But Abraham knew God was his source, no matter what things looked like to the naked eye. Abraham was saying, "It doesn't matter where I go, the Lord is going to bless me." Right after Abraham allowed Lot to take the better land, God appeared to him and promised even more prosperity than Abraham had already experienced.

> *The LORD said unto Abram, after that Lot was separated from him, Lift up now thine eyes, and look from the place where thou art northward, and southward, and eastward, and westward: For all the land which thou seest, to thee will I give it, and to thy seed for ever. And I will make thy seed as the dust of the earth: so that if a man can number the dust of the earth, then shall thy seed also be numbered. Arise, walk through the land in the length of it and in the breadth of it; for I will give it unto thee.*
>
> *Genesis 13:14–17*

In the natural, it is impossible for a man who grazes his flocks and herds in the desert to prosper as much as a man whose cattle graze in lush pastures, but nothing is impossible for God (Luke

1:37). The blessing of God made Abraham rich, and he prospered much more than Lot did.

Not long after Lot and Abraham separated, foreign kings raided the city of Sodom where Lot lived and took everyone captive. When Abraham heard that his nephew had been seized, he armed his servants that were trained for war and pursued the foreign kings. His party consisted of 318 men, which gives you an idea of how many servants he had (Genesis 14:14). Abraham's men defeated the foreign kings and brought back all of the spoil and the people who had been taken captive.

The king of Sodom was grateful, so he offered to let Abraham keep the spoil: "The king of Sodom said unto Abram, Give me the persons, and take the goods to thyself" (Genesis 14:21). The king recognized that if it hadn't been for Abraham, his entire kingdom would have been lost. We don't know how much spoil the king was offering Abraham, but it isn't unreasonable to think it would have been the equivalent of millions of dollars today. Abraham had recovered all the goods, food, and valuables of five cities, so the spoil was certainly worth a lot of money. But Abraham didn't accept the king's offer.

> *Abram said to the king of Sodom, I have lift up mine hand unto the LORD, the most high God, the possessor of heaven and earth, That I will not take from a thread even to a shoelatchet, and that I will not take any thing that is thine, lest thou shouldest say, I have made Abram rich: Save only that which the young men have eaten, and the portion of the men which*

*went with me, Aner, Eshcol, and Mamre; let them take their
portion.*

Genesis 14:22–24

Abraham refused to take any money from the king because he
didn't want anyone to have a reason to claim they had made him
rich. Abraham knew he was rich because of the blessing of God.
His confidence in God as the source of his wealth was so strong
that he gave away millions of dollars' worth of spoil, which he had
rightfully earned by conquest. Abraham had a lot of possessions and
many people working for him, but he saw himself as a recipient of
God's blessing—not as someone who was earning wealth through
his own efforts.

The foundation for Abraham's confidence goes back to when
God appeared to him and said, "I will bless you, and I will make
your name great." I'm sure Abraham put effort into maintaining
his flocks and herds, and he had hundreds of servants helping him,
but he still saw God as his source. He trusted in God, and because
of that, God prospered him supernaturally. This same attitude is
necessary for any Christian to really begin to walk in the financial
prosperity God desires for us.

We need to see God as our source and develop the attitude that
the resources we have are a gift from God. Yes, you may have worked
forty or sixty hours a week at your job, but God is the source! God
gave you life, health, and abilities, and God is the One who opens
doors of opportunity. God is our source, and just like Abraham, we
need to recognize that the money we have belongs to God.

After Abraham boldly declared that God was his source and gave away a fortune rather than give the king any basis for saying he made Abraham rich, the Lord appeared to Abraham in a vision and said, "Fear not, Abram: I am thy shield, and thy exceeding great reward" (Genesis 15:1). This statement had spiritual meaning, but it also had financial significance. Abraham gave away millions to preserve God as his sole source, but God gave back to Abraham even more financial increase. Abraham received from God an equivalent of all that bounty plus interest.

Until you recognize God as your source, nothing else the Bible says about finances is going to work. As long as you are holding onto your money with a clenched fist and hoarding possessions, God's method of prosperity won't work in your life. You have to change your mindset and recognize that God is the source of everything you own, seeing yourself as a steward managing the financial blessings that God has given you.

God is the source of your resources just as surely as He was Abraham's source. The difference is that Abraham knew God was his source, and his trust in God caused him to prosper. One of the reasons we don't see greater prosperity in our lives is that we haven't learned the lesson of being a steward. We see everything we own as being the result of our own sweat and tears and because of that, we have a stingy, selfish attitude toward money. The first step toward walking in financial prosperity is to recognize that you are not the source of your financial blessing.

> *One of the reasons we don't see greater prosperity in our lives is that we haven't learned the lesson of being a steward.*

Seeing God as your source doesn't mean you sit at home and do nothing. You are supposed to work, but you need to recognize that even though you work, it is God who gives the increase (1 Corinthians 3:7). A farmer has to prepare the soil and plant seeds in order to get a crop, but God created the natural laws that govern sowing and reaping, God sends the rain and sun that make plants grow, God gave the land to farm on, and God is the source of the farmer's health. Likewise, it is the blessing of God that makes it possible for you to prosper, and the foundation of prosperity is seeing yourself as a steward.

Chapter 2

God Is a Giver

Many people are afraid to loosen the death grip they have on their money because they think God will take it all away. Actually, God will treat you better than you treat yourself. God is El Shaddai,[2] not El Cheapo. He might make different choices than you would, but He will certainly treat you better.

The church has promoted so many wrong ideas over the years that people think the Lord wants Christians to live in little shacks with no money in our pockets. The Word of God says differently. God wants to bless His children. In fact, if you aren't embarrassed by your level of prosperity, then there is a good chance you aren't depending upon God as your source. I know that sounds a little shocking, but I believe it's true.

A man I used to know bought me cars for a number of years—and he didn't buy me cheap cars; he bought me top-of-the-line. He gave me a Chevy Suburban that was so nice that everywhere I

---

[2] "From *shadah*, to shed, to pour out. I am that God who pours out blessings, who gives them richly, abundantly, continually." Adam Clarke, *Adam Clarke's Commentary*, "Commentary on Genesis 17," available from http://www.studylight.org/com/acc/view.cgi?book=ge&chapter=017, S.V. "I am the Almighty God," Genesis 17:1.

went, people would ask me where I got it and what I did for a living. When they found out I was a preacher, the look on their face said, "This car is way too nice for a preacher." It got to be embarrassing for me to take the vehicle out in public.

Eventually, I went to the man who gave me the Suburban and said, "Look, I love this vehicle—and I'm not complaining—but it's embarrassing. People don't think a preacher should be driving something this nice." He looked at me for a moment and then said, "If you aren't embarrassed at your level of prosperity, then God isn't really your source." Those words went straight to my heart. It's true that if you can look at everything you have and say, "I did this; this is all the result of my effort," then you haven't tapped into God's supernatural ability—you're just depending on yourself.

Of course, godly prosperity is different from coveting riches. Yes, God wants you to have nice things, but you shouldn't get them by hoarding your money and spending it all on yourself. When you give and handle your assets like a steward of God's money, then God will bless you—and the blessing of God adds no sorrow with it. You'll have nice things, but you won't be in hock up to your eyeballs or working yourself sick.

When you open up your hand and begin to trust God, you'll see that God is not a taker—He's a multiplier. He has not come into your life to take from you. The Bible is full of stories of men and women whom God blessed and prospered—and they all had the attitude of a steward. They all recognized God as their source.

David is a good example of a steward. He wanted to build the Lord a temple, but God told him he couldn't. God wanted David's son, Solomon, to build the temple. David obeyed God, but he started setting aside the money and materials Solomon would need one day in order to build the temple. It was his way of contributing. David set aside the equivalent of $36 billion in gold and $14 billion in silver while Solomon was growing up. Then, right before he handed over the throne to Solomon, he made one last gift. He said,

> *Moreover, because I have set my affection to the house of my God, I have of mine own proper good, of gold and silver, which I have given to the house of my God, over and above all that I have prepared for the holy house. Even three thousand talents of gold, of the gold of Ophir, and seven thousand talents of refined silver, to overlay the walls of the houses withal: The gold for things of gold, and the silver for things of silver, and for all manner of work to be made by the hands of artificers. And who then is willing to consecrate his service this day unto the LORD?*
>
> *1 Chronicles 29:3–5*

For this one gift, David gave 110 tons of gold and 260 tons of silver. By today's prices, that is $6 billion in gold and over $300 million in silver.[3] After giving this huge gift, David encouraged other people to give. All the leaders of the tribes caught the spirit of giving and began to donate large sums of money. The leaders gave even more than David: 190 tons of gold and 375 tons of silver. All together, they gave $17 billion in gold and silver in that one day.

---

[3]Gold at $1,730 per ounce, and silver at $40 per ounce (at the time of this writing).

Wherefore David blessed the LORD before all the congregation: and David said, Blessed be thou, LORD God of Israel our father, for ever and ever. Thine, O LORD, is the greatness, and the power, and the glory, and the victory, and the majesty: for all that is in the heaven and in the earth is thine; thine is the kingdom, O LORD, and thou art exalted as head above all. Both riches and honour come of thee, and thou reignest over all; and in thine hand is power and might; and in thine hand it is to make great, and to give strength unto all.

1 Chronicles 29:10–12

David saw himself as a steward. He knew that all of his assets had been given to him by God. David gave God the credit for being the source of all his riches. God had taken the people of Israel out of slavery and made them a rich and prosperous nation, able to donate more than $16 billion in one day. God had made them great. Then David said,

O LORD our God, all this store that we have prepared to build thee an house for thine holy name cometh of thine hand, and is all thine own. I know also, my God, that thou triest the heart, and hast pleasure in uprightness. As for me, in the uprightness of mine heart I have willingly offered all these things: and now have I seen with joy thy people, which are present here, to offer willingly unto thee.

1 Chronicles 29:16–17

Notice how David said that they had only given what God first gave to them; all they had done was give back to God what was rightfully His anyway. This is the attitude I'm trying to describe.

In order to begin to prosper, you have to stop thinking of money as belonging to you. You need to quit seeing yourself as the source of your prosperity and recognize that all blessings and riches come from God.

The reason people are so stressed out about money is that they think they are in control of their finances. People tend to think they are responsible for all of the factors that lead to prosperity and the money needed to survive. They are worried about losing their jobs or a downturn in the economy because they see themselves as the source of their provision.

Seeing yourself as the source of blessing in your life puts a lot of pressure on you to control circumstances that are really beyond your control. One of the benefits of seeing yourself as a steward is peace of mind and a sense of security. When you know that God is your source, you aren't worried about the natural circumstances. If God can prosper Abraham and feed his flocks and herds in a desert, then He can bless and prosper you in any economic situation. It doesn't matter what is going on around you. God is responsible for you, and even has numbered all the hairs of your head (Matthew 10:30). The Lord meets our needs according to His

Seeing yourself as a steward brings peace of mind and a sense of security.

riches in glory, not this country's economy (Philippians 4:19). If you are stressed out about finances—maybe you are single and trying to figure out how to make ends meet, or you're married and arguing with your spouse about money—then I encourage you to start looking to God as the source of your prosperity. God will take better care of your finances than you can.

Sometimes it's hard to look beyond the physical or natural challenges you face and see into the spiritual realm, but you can do it with a steward's mentality. Being a steward gives you a sense of confidence that you will never have as long as you see yourself as your source. I'm telling you, adopting the attitude of a steward will really help you.

In my own life, I recognize that I am not the one who has caused my success. It isn't my great wisdom or ability that has caused our ministry to succeed; it's the blessing of God. I haven't forgotten the poverty that God lifted my wife, Jamie, and me out of. I know God is my source. I have resources, but it's not really my money—it's God's money, and I'm a steward.

My mother was ninety-six at her death in 2009. Just one month before she died, she asked me to tell her again all the things the Lord was doing through this ministry. I shared with her about changed lives all over the world. As I was going on and on about all the Lord was doing, she interrupted with, "Andy, you know this is God." I replied, "Yes, Mother, I know this is God." Then she said, "You aren't smart enough to do this." Wow! There is nothing like a mother to put you in your place!

But I totally agree. As I look back on my life and ministry, I could not have planned what has happened. I had a vision and desire planted by the Lord, but I didn't have a clue about how to bring it to pass. All Jamie and I have done is hold on to Jesus for dear life and the Lord has taken us on the most incredible journey. I truly see God as the source of all good things in our lives.

Every one of us needs to see our income as something God has entrusted us with, and then ask ourselves what God wants us to do with it. Knowing that your income is really God's money makes you approach finances with a totally different attitude—and your attitude toward money is actually more important than what you do with it.

Look at what is written in the book of Psalms about attitude.

Hear, O my people, and I will speak; O Israel, and I will testify against thee: I am God, even thy God. I will not reprove thee for thy sacrifices or thy burnt offerings, to have been continually before me. I will take no bullock out of thy house, nor he goats out of thy folds. For every beast of the forest is mine, and the cattle upon a thousand hills. I know all the fowls of the mountains: and the wild beasts of the field are mine. If I were hungry, I would not tell thee: for the world is mine, and the fulness thereof. Will I eat the flesh of bulls, or drink the blood of goats? Offer unto God thanksgiving; and pay thy vows unto the most High.

Psalm 50:7–14

God was saying that His disagreement with them wasn't about a lack of sacrifices on their part; they had been offering sacrifices continually. His complaint against them was the heart attitude they had in making the offerings. They were missing the point! God didn't need the sacrifices. In instituting the sacrificial system, He was trying to illustrate the need for blood to be spilled in order for men to be made righteous (Romans 5:9). It was a prophetic foreshadowing of how Christ would offer His blood in payment for our sins. It was a type and shadow of a future New Testament reality. The Israelites were going through the motions of making the offerings, but they weren't giving their hearts to God.

They thought they were making sacrifices because God somehow needed their bulls and goats. In this scripture, God was making it clear that He didn't need anything from them; everything already belongs to the Lord. God said, "If I were hungry, I wouldn't tell you! The world is mine, and everything in it." He doesn't need to ask anyone for food. The truth was that the Israelites needed those sacrifices. They needed to give back to God and show their trust and dependence upon Him. It wasn't for God—it was for them.

Do you know why God asked us to give 10 percent of our income to the church? It isn't because God needs our money! All of the gold, silver, and riches in the earth already belong to Him (Haggai 2:8). He doesn't need our donations. God could have set up church finances differently. He could have made every minister of the Gospel independently wealthy like He made Abraham, Isaac, David, Solomon, and all the rest. The tithe exists for our benefit, not God's.

God doesn't need your money any more than He needed those Old Testament sacrifices. The point of the tithe is for you to learn to recognize God as the source of all of your money. It's one thing to say you believe God is your source, but it's another thing to prove it. The way you prove to yourself—not God—that you believe God is your source is to give a portion of what you make back to Him. People who don't really see God as their source are going to balk at giving part of what they have away. They are going to think, *I need that money!* But giving back some of what God has already given you is nothing when you see God as your source.

Money is difficult to come by when you think of yourself as the provider. Money reminds you of how hard you have to work just to get by, and giving it away would only seem to put you further away from the goal of having all your needs met. All of that would be true if God wasn't your source. In God's economy, you move closer toward your goals by giving than you do by clinging to everything you have.

It all comes down to faith, and that's why God told us to give. He doesn't need our money. God could establish His kingdom using other principles. He could give every person in ministry creative ideas that would generate incredible wealth. He could have done all sorts of things, but God set up His kingdom around giving because He wants you to trust Him and recognize Him as your source. He wants you to remember that even though you have money, you didn't get it by your own power. Moses wrote,

> *Thou shalt remember the Lord thy God: for it is he that giveth thee power to get wealth, that he may establish his covenant which he sware unto thy fathers, as it is this day.*

> *Deuteronomy 8:18*

God gives us the power to get wealth, and it's important for us to recognize that He is our source—regardless of how much effort we put into earning a living. All prosperity comes from God. He blesses us so that "he may establish his covenant," and so we can be a blessing to others. Yes, God gives you money to survive and pay your bills, but the primary reason He has blessed you is so that you can be a blessing (Genesis 12:3; Ephesians 4:28; 2 Corinthians 9:8).

Giving is a problem when you see yourself as the owner of your finances because when God leads you to give, or when you see instructions in the Word that tell you to give, you may start thinking, *What right does God have to tell me what to do with my own money?* But the truth is that whatever wealth you have came from God. He is the One who gives you the power and ability to prosper.

The interesting thing about this scripture in Deuteronomy 8:18 is that God was talking to the children of Israel who would eventually enter into the Promised Land. They were going to be living in homes built for giants. The fields already had the rocks cleared out of them, the furrows were dug, and the crops were planted. The Israelites were going to step in and benefit from the labor of others. God was telling them not to forget the source of their wealth when they went from living in the desert to living in mansions with abundant prosperity. In context, God was saying, "Don't think you got wealthy by your own might or power. I'm the One who made you rich, and I did it to establish My covenant upon the earth."

The same is true for us today. God is the One who makes us wealthy. I know a lot of people don't feel wealthy, but that is partly because our standards for wealth are a little out of balance in the developed world. We are prosperous so far beyond our physical needs that people don't feel like they have enough unless they drive a brand-new luxury car and own five flat-screen televisions. Our level of poverty doesn't even compare to what most people on this earth have lived through. Most of us have no idea what it means to struggle to survive.

We live at a level of relative prosperity that most people throughout history couldn't have dreamed of, yet we didn't do anything to be born at this time. We didn't cause ourselves to be born into such opportunity and freedom. Even today, some people are born into social systems that don't permit them to seek prosperity, or into dictatorships that control their financial status. Others have suffered through war, persecution, and imprisonment. We are super blessed to be born into such a time of prosperity. It should help us see that the ability to prosper is a gift from God, and we can't boast of the opportunities we have been given.

The apostle Paul talked about that in his letter to the Corinthian church. He said,

For who maketh thee to differ from another? and what hast thou that thou didst not receive? now if thou didst receive it, why dost thou glory, as if thou hadst not received it?

1 Corinthians 4:7

Everything we have has been given to us by God, and since we received it, there is no room for boasting that we earned it. The Corinthians worked just like we do, but Paul still said that everything they were and all that they had, came from God. I have probably spent tens of thousands of hours studying the Word, but it would be wrong for me to adopt the attitude that I am a self-made man. I have worked to make sure our ministry does well, but I am not the reason it is successful. God called me into the ministry and blessed me with success by His grace, not because of anything I have done.

Many Christians recognize God as the cause of professional success, but far fewer people make the connection that God is also the source of financial success. A lot of people see the hand of God in granting them professional opportunities, but the truth is that you don't have a single thing that God didn't give you. What gets you into financial trouble is failing to recognize your role as a steward of God's resources. A steward knows that his master wouldn't want him to go into debt and pay two or three times the actual value of something in interest. Stewards don't make impulse purchases because they just can't wait to get a new toy, and they don't mortgage their future to buy things on credit.

The Word of God is full of instructions to help us make good financial decisions. For instance, the Word tells us to set money aside and be prepared. The reason a little dip in finances devastates a lot of people is that they don't have any savings, and often it's because they haven't made the best use of their money. Some people have plenty of money coming in, but they are living so close to the limit that it only takes a slight economic downturn to send them into financial disaster. Following God's financial advice will save you from making those mistakes, but you have to adopt the mindset of a steward before you can understand what the Word says about managing money.

It's possible to prosper without God, but it comes with heartache. The Word says that the blessing of the Lord makes you rich, and

He adds no sorrow with it (Proverbs 10:22). When you're doing it all yourself, you carry the load of responsibility also. That's why people are so stressed out about what's going to happen in the stock market, or how they're going to pay their bills. When God is your source there is no sorrow added to your prosperity. Scripture says,

They that will be rich fall into temptation and a snare, and into many foolish and hurtful lusts, which drown men in destruction and perdition. For the love of money is the root of all evil: which while some coveted after, they have erred from the faith, and pierced themselves through with many sorrows.

1 Timothy 6:9–10

The way the world goes about trying to prosper is ungodly, and those who gain prosperity in an ungodly way bring grief upon themselves. The world's attitude toward finances is causing people to be totally stressed out. They need a pill to get through the day and another pill to get to sleep at night. We need to quit following the example of the world. The godly way to seek prosperity is to remember that God has given us the power to get wealth, and our role is to be stewards of what God has blessed us with. We seek first of all God's kingdom and He adds all the physical things we need to us (Matthew 6:33).

The two most important steps toward prosperity are to realize that God is your source and to develop the mindset of a steward. Once you do those two things, the Word of God will cause you to prosper. It also takes away the stress and worry associated with finances, because it's not your money! You don't have to fear that God is going to take from you if you loosen your grip on money.

God is a multiplier, not a subtracter. The fact is that being a steward puts everything into perspective and enables you to receive greater blessings from God. You'll be blessed, and you'll be a greater blessing to other people.

Chapter 3

Greater Things

He that is faithful in that which is least is faithful also in much: and he that is unjust in the least is unjust also in much.

Luke 16:10

People use this scripture to say that if you want to be entrusted with a lot of authority, then you have to start small and work your way up. I even tell the students I teach at Charis Bible College that you aren't going to leave school and jump right into pastoring a church of a thousand members. You have to be faithful in the small things first—serving at your church, teaching a Bible study, and other ministry work. As you become faithful through doing small things, God will increase your leadership responsibilities. Those are true statements, and it isn't wrong to use this scripture to demonstrate that truth, but it isn't really what Jesus was talking about here.

Jesus said that money is the least area of trusting God.

The context of a scripture determines its main application, and the context of this scripture is the steward who had wasted his master's money. In context, Jesus is saying that the least area of trusting God is money. What an incredible statement! It is also completely contrary to the way most believers think.

Many think that money is something for mature Christians to deal with and that salvation and living a holy life are the simple things. As a matter of fact, somebody always gets upset with me when I teach about finances on television or radio. I actually received a letter one time from a listener who threatened to sue me for wasting airtime talking about money. He was absolutely livid that I would take time to talk about finances when I should—he thought—be talking about more important issues. But finances are the least area of trusting God! It's a starting place. In the parable of the unjust steward, Jesus went on to say:

> *If therefore ye have not been faithful in the unrighteous*
> *mammon, who will commit to your trust the true riches? And*
> *if ye have not been faithful in that which is another man's,*
> *who shall give you that which is your own? No servant can*
> *serve two masters: for either he will hate the one, and love*
> *the other; or else he will hold to the one, and despise the other.*
> *Ye cannot serve God and mammon.*

Luke 16:11–13

Mammon means money.[4] We need to talk about money because Jesus said in this parable that trusting God in the area of finances is the least area of trust, and you can't do greater things without doing the lesser things first. If you can't lift five pounds, then you certainly shouldn't go out and try to lift a hundred pounds. You

---

[4]Thayer and Smith, *The KJV New Testament Greek Lexicon*, "Greek Lexicon entry for Mammonas," available from http://www.biblestudytools.com/lexicons/greek/kjv/mammonas.html, S.V. "mammon," Luke 16:13.

have to start with what is least and work your way up. If you can't walk ten paces, then you can't climb a mountain. If you can't run a mile, then you can't run a marathon. When you start an exercise program, you don't start with the greatest; you start with that which is least and work your way up.

Remember, Jesus is saying that trusting God with your finances is the least area of trusting God. It's the least use of your faith. When Jesus said in Luke 16:10, "He that is faithful in that which is least," He was calling money "that which is least." Think about it: *If you aren't trusting God in your finances, then you are deceiving yourself to think you are trusting Him with your eternal salvation—or anything else.* That is profound!

If you aren't seeing greater things come to pass in your life, the reason may very well be that you aren't trusting God with "that which is least." Believing for your family to be restored, for healing to manifest in your body, or for mental and emotional healing are all infinitely greater than believing for finances. If you haven't started trusting God with your finances yet, how can you go beyond that and trust Him to heal your body? How will you trust God to get over depression if you can't do that which is least and trust Him with your money? How can you trust God to give you eternal life but not trust Him to provide for your physical needs?

Clinging to money out of fear that God won't provide for you but then trying to say you are believing God for healing or restoration is like saying, "I can't jump three feet, but I'm going to jump clear across the Grand Canyon." It just doesn't work that way. It isn't that God wants you to jump through a bunch of hoops before He will heal you—no, everything has already been provided.[5] It's because you probably won't be able to trust God for big things until you can trust Him for little things first.

Trusting God with our finances is much more important than it has been given credit for being. Many people are trying to bypass this issue and move on to bigger things, but it won't work. Just like other areas of life, you have to start at the beginning and work your way up. You can't jump from the ground to the top of a ladder. You have to start at the bottom rung and work your way up. Trusting God with your finances is the bottom rung. It's the starting place.

I taught this same message at a church in California one time, and God used it to really touch people's hearts. After I taught, I received an offering to give them an opportunity to act on what they had learned. I didn't want them to think I was doing it for selfish reasons, so I gave the entire offering to the pastor of the church. As they were passing the buckets, the Lord spoke to me and said, "Watch what happens now that these people have started trusting me with their finances." When the offering was finished, I stood up to pray, and miracles started happening! People started receiving the healing power of God. It was such a dramatic demonstration of God's power that people were running to the front asking what they needed to do to be saved.

I saw with my own eyes that the reason some of those people hadn't been healed was because they had never fully trusted God

---

[5]God provided healing, deliverance, salvation, and prosperity through His Son, Jesus, 2,000 years ago. These gifts become a reality for us when we mix them with faith because faith appropriates what God has already provided.

in the area of finances. I know that a lot of ministers don't see things this way. They want to just preach about salvation and leave Christians to try to figure out finances on their own, but that isn't what Scripture teaches. Jesus said that trusting God with our finances is foundational.

Please don't misunderstand me. I'm not saying that if you just give money then you will receive a miracle. You can't buy healing or any other blessing of God. You can only receive from God by faith. Faith is the only thing that makes anything God has done for us manifest in our lives. What I am saying is that using your faith for finances is the least use of faith, and if you haven't done that which is least, then you won't be able to do greater things.

I meet people all of the time who are seeking physical and emotional healing, but they haven't started trusting God with their money yet. Honestly, I'm probably not as bold in telling people about this as I should be. I should probably be stronger about this because I know in my heart that people have come to me wanting to receive healing for cancer from God when they have never started believing His simple promises concerning giving and receiving. They don't give or tithe because they don't really believe that God's promises about financial provision are true. They don't really trust God. So

Using your faith for finances is the least use of faith, and if you haven't done that which is least, then you won't be able to do greater things.

how are they going to trust Him to heal them of cancer? They won't believe God for the greater thing if they won't believe Him for money, which is the least use of our faith.

45

On a few occasions, I have questioned people about their giving. I remember a friend of mine who came to one of my meetings in Atlanta asking me for prayer. As we were talking, the Lord quickened to me that she hadn't been giving. This was a Christian who knew better, and so I asked her, "Have you been faithful in your giving?

She looked at me and then said, "No, I fell behind and I haven't been doing it."

She was trying to believe God for healing, yet she wasn't doing that which is least. So I told her, "Until you start acting on what you already know and using your faith for those smaller things, there is no point in me praying for you to receive bigger things."

Some people might be shocked that I would tie being faithful in your finances to receiving healing from God, but those things can be connected. It's not a matter of pleasing God with giving before He will heal you. It's all about being able to trust Him for small things before you try trusting Him for big things. Jesus said the exact same thing when the rich young ruler came to Him and said, "What shall I do to inherit eternal life?" (Luke 18:18). Jesus recognized that the young man's heart wasn't right, so He told him to sell everything he had, give the proceeds to the poor, and then come follow Him. In essence, He was telling the young man, "If you can't trust Me in that which is least, then you won't trust Me for that which is greater."

In the parable we looked at earlier of the unjust steward, Jesus said, "If therefore ye have not been faithful in the unrighteous mammon, who will commit to your trust the true riches?" (Luke 16:11). People talk about money being true riches, but money is nothing compared to health. People pay millions of dollars trying to get well. Anyone who has ever been really sick can tell you that good health is priceless.

Some people are thinking that once they get healed, or after their marriage is restored, or after they are delivered from depression, *then* they will start being a faithful steward of their finances. They want to receive a greater blessing before they start trusting God for the lesser blessings. You can't do that. You have to start with that which is least and work your way up.

It would be foolish to try to believe God for the healing of cancer and yet not trust Him with your finances. At the very least, you are going to be frustrated and disappointed if you don't see your physical body healed. Or worse, you might become bitter and think faith doesn't work or that God's Word isn't true. No, faith works and God wants you well, but faith is trust in God. If you don't trust God with your finances, then you probably won't be able to trust that His Son, Jesus, has already paid the price for your healing. Remember, the Word says that you can't serve two masters (Luke 16:13). You can't trust yourself when it comes to money and then try to trust God with everything else.

I'm not saying these things to hurt anyone—I'm saying it to enlighten you. If you have been standing in faith for healing but you haven't seen any physical manifestation, this could be the reason. Think about how you handle your finances: Are you trusting God with your finances? If not, then you don't need to look any further for why you haven't received healing. It isn't effective to compartmentalize your faith so that you are trying to trust God in one area, but not in others. If you are going to trust God, then trust Him all the way. The same God who promised eternal life when you confess Jesus as your Lord, and believe in your heart that God raised Him from the dead (Romans 10:9), also said to give and it would be given back to you (Luke 6:38).

Imagine if I had the resources to guarantee that I could give $1,000 back to everyone who sent me $10. If you really believed that I was telling the truth, then you would be foolish not to send me $10. It wouldn't matter what kind of financial straits you were in; you could find $10. If you really and truly believed that I was a man of my word, then it would be ridiculous not to invest $10 in order to receive $1,000 back. Even if you were living on the street, you would find a way to get me $10. I think everyone can understand that. Well, Jesus said the same thing in Scripture: "Give, and it shall be given unto you; good measure, pressed down, and shaken together, and running over, shall men give into your bosom" (Luke 6:38).

Jesus also said that anyone who sacrifices home or family will be rewarded with one hundred times what they sacrificed *in this life,* as well as the gift of eternal life (Mark 10:30). If you haven't been giving but you really believe God's promises, then why wouldn't you give of your finances and trust that He will give back much more than you gave? One of God's promises, as we just saw, is that He will give back to you abundantly, so if you aren't giving, you don't really believe the promises of God.

I could cite a lot of verses that talk about God blessing us and prospering us when we give; it's an established principle in the Word of God. People are deceiving themselves when they say that they are trusting and believing in God but they aren't giving financially. If you aren't giving to God, then you either don't know His promises to give back to you or you don't really believe those promises are true.

Lack of trust in finances will hinder your entire walk with the Lord. Let me put it this way: I don't know a single mature Christian who doesn't tithe and give. Everyone I know who has made a total commitment to the Lord trusts God with their finances. On the other hand, I could give you many examples of people who don't trust God with their finances, and their relationship with God is up and down like a yo-yo. They haven't learned to trust God in their finances, and they have no stability in their lives. The conclusion I draw is that people who don't trust God with their finances are not mature, stable Christians—and won't become stable until they start trusting God in this area.

One reason so many Christians are stuck in their walk with the Lord is that they haven't started trusting God in the area of finances.

If that describes you, just keep in mind that sowing and reaping takes time. Likewise, learning to trust God with your finances and moving into maturity and stability in this area is a process.

This isn't just for the people who want to be fanatics. This is for baby (or new) Christians. You cannot truly mature and fully walk in the blessings of God until you start trusting Him with your finances. As we just saw, the same God who promised that He would save you and give you eternal life also promised to prosper you financially. It's double-minded (James 1:7–8) to say that you will trust God with your eternal salvation but not trust Him enough to give and see yourself as a steward of God's resources.

Prosperity is a part of our salvation. The Word says that Jesus became poor so that we, through His poverty, might be made rich (2 Corinthians 8:9). Some people try to spiritualize that verse and say it is talking about being rich emotionally, but the context of the verse is finances. Yes, Jesus came to make us rich emotionally and spiritually, but He also came to provide for our physical needs. Jesus became poor so that we could be made rich.

We can't just pick and choose which portions of the Word we are going to believe. Don't listen to those who try to spiritualize every scripture about finances and pretend like money doesn't matter—it does matter. In fact, Jesus told the rich young ruler that if he couldn't trust God for his financial needs, then he wouldn't trust God for his salvation (Luke 18:18–25). We touched on this story earlier, but the point is that Jesus used finances to demonstrate to that young man the true condition of his heart. Remember, Jesus said that if we aren't faithful in that which is least, then we won't be faithful in something greater (Luke 16:10). Trusting God with your finances is where you start. Let's take an in-depth look at the story of the rich young ruler.

> *When he was gone forth into the way, there came one*
> *running, and kneeled to him, and asked him, Good Master,*
> *what shall I do that I may inherit eternal life? And Jesus said*
> *unto him, Why callest thou me good? there is none good but*
> *one, that is, God.*

Mark 10:17–18

Sometimes we read through Scripture without thinking about it enough to let it have its full impact on us. Try to picture the situation here. Jesus was a radical and controversial figure in His day. The scribes and Pharisees had established that anyone who acknowledged Jesus as the Messiah was going to be kicked out of the synagogue, so there was persecution for those who associated with Jesus. Yet, this rich young man ran and fell at the feet of Jesus saying, "Good Master, what shall I do that I may inherit eternal life?"

This young man had some degree of commitment to fall down at Jesus' feet like that. He could have been kicked out of the synagogue. He certainly would have been ridiculed. It was a big deal for him to publicly acknowledge Jesus the way he did. Imagine yourself sitting in one of my meetings when all of a sudden somebody runs up and throws himself down at my feet and says, "How do I get saved?" Most people would think, "Wow, this guy is really sincere." But Jesus recognized that the young man wasn't all that he appeared to be. He wasn't really willing to commit himself to the Lord, even though he made such a public demonstration.

Man looks on the outward appearance, but the Lord looks on the heart (1 Samuel 16:7). Jesus was God in the flesh, and He wasn't moved by outward appearances. The young man's actions looked good, but his heart was wrong, and Jesus knew it, so He said, "Why are you calling me good?" In those days, "master" was just a term of respect, similar to the way we use *Mr.* or *Mrs.* It didn't mean the young man was submitting to Jesus. Jesus essentially said, "Look, you're calling Me a good master, but you have to go beyond that. You have to receive Me as Lord and accept Me as God. So either call Me God or quit calling Me good!"

Jesus had to be God in order for His sacrifice to be able to atone for the young man's sin. One man's sacrifice isn't worth any more than one man's life. For Jesus to be the Savior of the entire world, He had to be more than a mere man; He had to be God manifest in the flesh (1 Timothy 3:16). Jesus had been saying that He was God. He called Himself God and referred to Himself as the Son of God. He also said that we have to honor Him exactly the way we honor the Father (John 5:23), but the young man wasn't honoring Jesus as God.

Some people today are saying Jesus was a great prophet, but they don't acknowledge Him as the Son of God. Others want to promote Jesus as a great example of love, but not as God. This is the exact same attitude the rich young ruler had. Contrary to those views, Jesus said, "I am the way, the truth, and the life: no man cometh unto the Father, but by me" (John 14:6). Jesus was either the Son of God or He was a liar—there are no other options. Our options today are the same ones the young ruler had: either make Jesus God or quit calling Him good!

Here's what the young ruler decided to do: "[The young ruler] answered and said unto [Jesus], Master, all these have I observed from my youth" (Mark 10:20). That young man dropped the *good!*

See, he never believed that Jesus was God manifest in the flesh. He believed that Jesus could offer something he wanted, but he wasn't willing to humble himself and acknowledge Jesus as his Lord. So Jesus told the young man to keep the commandments, and the young man had the audacity to say that he had kept them all from his youth (v. 20). Nobody has ever observed all of the commandments (Romans 3:23).

The New Testament reveals that it's not only your actions that count, but what is in your heart. If you've been angry with a person without cause, you're guilty of murder (Matthew 5:21–22). If you have lusted after a person or coveted what they own, then you're guilty of lust, adultery, and covetousness (vv. 27–28). So it's not just whether you physically go out and disobey the commandments. According to Scripture, if you've lusted for these things in your heart, then you're guilty.

This young man was deceiving himself to think he had kept all of the commandments. I believe one of the main reasons the Lord told him to go sell everything he had and give it to the poor was because the first commandment is "Thou shalt have no other gods before me" (Exodus 20:3). This man's wealth was his god. He would rather have his money and what his money could buy than have God. He wanted all of his money because he coveted the things money could get him, which violates the last commandment: "Thou shalt not covet" (v. 17). I believe Jesus was showing the man that he had broken the first and the last commandments, and probably everything in between. Look how Jesus responded after the man claimed to have kept all of the commandments.

Then Jesus beholding him loved him, and said unto him, One thing thou lackest: go thy way, sell whatsoever thou hast, and give to the poor, and thou shalt have treasure in heaven: and come, take up the cross, and follow me.

Mark 10:21

Jesus loved the young man. He didn't say these things because He was mad. He wasn't trying to hurt him or drive him away by giving him an impossible task. No, Jesus loved this man and wanted to help him. In his heart, the man was trusting in money, and Jesus was trying to help him shift his trust to God.

You may be experiencing financial difficulties and you might be thinking that I've been insensitive because of some of the things I have said about trusting God with your finances. If you are financially challenged, maybe it seems like I don't understand just how hard your situation is or like I don't care. But I do care; that's the reason I wrote this book! I'm trying to help raise you up out of poverty and financial crisis. I'm trying to help you shift your trust to the Lord so that you can start receiving prosperity by faith instead of depending on yourself and stressing yourself out. It's the exact same motivation Jesus had with the rich man.

When the young man heard Jesus ask him to sell everything he had and give the proceeds to the poor, he hung his head and walked away. He knew in his heart that he couldn't do it. After the man left, the disciples began asking Jesus questions about what He had just taught on money. Finally, Jesus said to them:

> *Verily I say unto you, There is no man that hath left house, or brethren, or sisters, or father, or mother, or wife, or children, or lands, for my sake, and the gospel's, But he shall receive an hundredfold now in this time, houses, and brethren, and sisters, and mothers, and children, and lands, with persecutions; and in the world to come eternal life.*
>
> *Mark 10:29–30*

Jesus said this right after they saw the rich man walk away. In other words, if the man had sold everything he had and given it to the poor, he would have received a hundredfold return in this life. Jesus wasn't trying to take from the man. He would have blessed him back a hundred times over. You're a steward, and the money you have isn't really yours anyway, but God is never going to let you outgive Him. When you do give, the Lord will always bless you back—not just in heaven, but here on earth too.

The rich man's refusal to sell his possessions revealed the true condition of his heart. His trust in money was a hindrance to his relationship with God—money was his god. Likewise, if some of the things I am saying rub you the wrong way, it may be that your heart isn't right in this matter. Just as Jesus used money to reveal the rich man's attitude, you can see what is in a person's heart by looking at how they operate financially.

Jesus didn't ask every rich person He met to sell everything they owned. He went to the house of a very wealthy tax collector named Zacchaeus and never mentioned money—and tax collectors earned a lot of money by stealing from people (Luke 19:2–9). Zacchaeus decided to give half of his goods to the poor and to restore four times any money he had stolen, but Jesus didn't ask him to do those things; Zacchaeus did them voluntarily. Jesus didn't ask everyone to sell all they had because the issue isn't money—it's whether or not you are trusting money instead of God.

God gives us money because we need it to function in this world. We use it to buy the goods that meet our needs, but money is not what provides for us. The question is whether we are trusting in God as the source of our provision, or whether we are operating out of fear and trusting in money itself. Money is just a delivery system; God is our source.

A lot of Christians say, "My trust is in the Lord," but you can tell where their heart really is by looking at how they give. Are they faithful givers, or are they hoarding everything they get? Jesus told the rich man to sell everything he had in an effort to reveal the condition of his heart. If Jesus was still on earth in His physical body today, He would be asking whether our trust is in God or in stocks, bonds, and pension funds. He would be urging us to administer our finances as stewards and to put our trust in God.

God doesn't ask for tithes and offerings because He needs your money. He asks because He wants you to learn to trust Him with all of your heart, and finances are the first step in that direction.

The desire of God's heart is to be involved in every area of your life. He doesn't just want to be part of one hour a week at church. He doesn't want just a scrap of time every once in a while. He wants all of you, and the most dominant area of your life is the forty, fifty, or sixty hours a week you spend earning a living. The way God gets you to trust Him in that area of your life is by asking you to give a portion of what you earn back to Him, and He promises to bless you back in return. It helps you remember that the power to get wealth comes from God, and it teaches you to trust God as your true source of prosperity.

Many people will not follow the leading of God because they are afraid—especially when it comes to earning income—but you have to believe God. You have to trust that God has your best interests at heart and that He will prosper and take care of you. Finances are the least use of your faith. This isn't for the "super saints." Baby Christians should start with trusting God in their finances. One reason is that you won't have the confidence to step out and do the things that God has called you to do until you can trust Him to be your source.

Sometimes we're afraid to step out and do what God is leading us to do, but the blessing on our life is in doing what God has called us to do. When my wife, Jamie, and I really started to step out and trust God with our finances, we saw the Lord come through for us time and time again. I could easily spend hours telling stories of God's miraculous financial provision in my life. I'm telling you, it did something for me that I can't verbalize when I began to see God supernaturally prosper us and lift us out of poverty. My faith in God went through the roof. I believe an important part of seeing my own son raised from the dead, and the countless other miracles I've seen, was learning to trust God in the area of finances. If I hadn't done that which is least, I couldn't have seen those greater things come to pass. That can be true for you too.

Chapter 4

Hidden Treasure

L ooking at the world around us, we can see that money has power. It obviously enables us to do things we can't otherwise do, and it gives us a certain level of respect. For instance, when a rich man walks into a room, his financial status gives him authority that a poor person in the same room doesn't have. The danger is that unless you are careful, you will begin to trust more in the power of money than you do in the power of God. The Lord is aware of this temptation and that is why He said so many things about finances. In one of His teachings, Jesus said,

> *Lay not up for yourselves treasures upon earth, where moth and rust doth corrupt, and where thieves break through and steal: But lay up for yourselves treasures in heaven, where neither moth nor rust doth corrupt, and where thieves do not break through nor steal: For where your treasure is, there will your heart be also.*

> *Matthew 6:19–21*

The last verse in this passage is interesting. It says that your heart is where your treasure is—which means you can tell where a person's heart is by where their money goes! This scripture illustrates the point Jesus was making with the rich young ruler when He told the man to sell all of his goods (Mark 10:21). Jesus was saying, "If you really love and trust Me more than your money, then put your treasure in heaven." The man wouldn't do it because his treasure—and his heart—were in earthly riches. Of course, we know that the Lord would have blessed that man back with even more riches than he gave away, so God wasn't trying to take from him. Jesus was just trying to get the man to put his total trust and dependence on God.

The church doesn't preach on finances today the way Jesus did. Very little is being taught from the pulpit about money, and usually, when something is said, the motivation is to get us to give to fund ministries or projects. The primary message in any teaching on finances should be that if you aren't faithful in that which is least, you won't be faithful in that which is greater.

After the rich man walked away unwilling to part with his money, the Lord said:

> *How hardly shall they that have riches enter into the kingdom of God! And the disciples were astonished at his words. But Jesus answereth again, and saith unto them, Children, how hard is it for them that trust in riches to enter into the kingdom of God!*

Mark 10:23–24

You could say it this way: "How hard it is for rich people to be born again." That's quite a statement, which is why the disciples were astonished. But Jesus clarified His meaning by saying, "How hard it is for them that trust in riches." He wasn't saying that money itself makes it difficult to be saved. He was saying that having lots of money can trick people into putting faith in their money, instead of in God. Money isn't the problem—where you put your trust is the issue.

Are you putting your trust in money or in the Lord? It's a question everyone should ask themselves. All of us want to say, "Oh yeah, I'm trusting in the Lord," but you have to do more than just say it. As the apostle James said in his epistle, "Faith without works is dead" (James 2:26). So, yes, you can see where a person's heart is by where their money goes. Someone who is really trusting in the Lord will prove it by tithing and giving out of their resources. Again, the issue isn't money—it's where you put your trust. Whatever you serve becomes your master (Romans 6:16), and putting your trust in finances places you in bondage to money.

While serving money enslaves you, the Bible is full of evidence that God freely blesses His servants. Isaac was so prosperous that a king asked him to leave the land because it couldn't sustain his wealth (Genesis 26:16). Jacob was even more prosperous than Abraham or Isaac (Genesis 30:43). David started life as the runt of his family; his main responsibility was tending his father's sheep, but eventually, God made him king of Israel (1 Samuel 16:1, 11–13). David became so wealthy that he gave a $6 billion dollar offering in one day toward the building of the Temple (1 Chronicles 29:1–5). His son, Solomon, was even more prosperous (1 Kings 1:37).

The Lord knows how dependent we are upon money. He knows how fearful we can be about finances. People recognize that money gives them power. It enables them to put food on the table and pay their bills, so they see giving money away as losing power. They think they are losing leverage in life by giving. But God knows our frame (Psalm 103:14); He knows we are prone to fear in the area of finances, and that's the reason He made so many promises to prosper us when we trust in Him.

Once you step out and begin trusting God, realizing that finances are the least use of your faith, you will start to see God's supernatural provision. It will increase your faith, and you will begin believing God for bigger and better things. On the other hand, if you never learn to trust God with your finances, you are always going to have a lack of confidence in Him. At some point, when you find yourself in a tough situation, you'll try to stand on God's promises for a miracle, and it won't come to pass because you have lingering doubts. Your own heart may condemn you and say, *"You never believed God's promises like 'Give, and it shall be given unto you,'[6] so how can you trust the words on this page about healing? What really makes you think that by Jesus' stripes you are healed?"[7]*

Notice I didn't say God will condemn you—condemnation doesn't come from God. God doesn't withhold His miracle-working power from you based on your performance or history of giving. But if you are condemning yourself, and your heart is divided about whether or not God really desires good for you, then you are going to have a hard time believing in Him—and faith is how we receive from God. See, the danger with money is that you can get to where you trust in what money can do for you more than you trust in God. Then, when you come upon a problem that money

---

[6] Luke 6:38.
[7] 1 Peter 2:24.

can't solve, it will feel like the earth is crumbling beneath you. God will still be there to help you, but you won't have learned to trust in His ability to deliver you. This is a major reason why giving is important: because learning to trust God starts with your finances.

Another word for trust is *reliance*. To rely on something is to depend on it. The *Century Dictionary* defines *reliance* as "confident rest for support," as in, "We may have perfect reliance on the promises of God."[8] That's what the word *trust* means. What are you relying on? Are you relying on your money, or are you relying on God? Thinking, *I want to give, but I can't. I need this money,* means your confidence is in riches.

After Jesus told His disciples that it is hard to enter the kingdom of God when your trust is in riches, He said,

> *It is easier for a camel to go through the eye of a needle, than for a rich man to enter into the kingdom of God. And they were astonished out of measure, saying among themselves, Who then can be saved?*

> *Mark 10:25–26*

The disciples were shocked before, but this statement put them over the top. Now they were thinking no one could be saved! Jesus said it is easier for a camel to go through the eye of a needle than it is for a man who trusts in riches to be saved. He was stressing the importance of turning our finances over to God and trusting Him as our source, yet many people today are not acknowledging the emphasis that Jesus put on trusting God with our finances.

---

[8] *Century Dictionary Online*, available from www.global-language.com/ CENTURY, S.V. "reliance."

A popular story has circulated that tries to reinterpret what Jesus meant in this teaching. You may have heard the story yourself. Supposedly, the *eye of the needle* was a special gate in the city of Jerusalem. During the day, the story goes, big gates in the walls of the city were open, but at night the big gates were closed and the only way into the city was through a small opening in the gate. Supposedly, the smaller door was called the *eye of the needle* and in order to get a camel through, they had to unburden the camel and make it crawl through on its knees. In other words, getting a camel through "the eye of a needle" was hard work, but it wasn't impossible. It's a neat story, but no such gate existed.

Actually, I have a funny story about that. When I was in Israel, I asked our tour guide to show us "the eye-of-the-needle gate." At first, the guide told me that it was out of the way, and we didn't have time to go see it. I kept asking him about it, and he continued brushing me off. Finally, I asked him, "Is there really a gate called the eye of the needle?"

"No," he said, "there isn't." I asked him why he didn't just tell me that in the first place and he explained how the tour guides in Israel are trained to make sure tourists have a wonderful experience—not necessarily to tell them the truth.

The guide told me how one time he had a tour group that kept asking him to see the burning bush from the story of Moses (Exodus 3:1–3). He remembered a bush catching fire the week before behind a gas station, so he had the bus driver stop at the station. They all got off the bus and he told the tourists that the charred plant behind the gas station was Moses' burning bush! He said the tourists were lining up to take pictures next to it. They actually believed it was the same bush that burned in front of Moses thousands of years before—never mind that the whole reason Moses turned aside to inspect the bush was that it wasn't being consumed by the flames.

The *eye of the needle* wasn't a gate any more than some burned plant behind a gas station was Moses' burning bush. Jesus was literally talking about the eye of a needle. He wasn't saying it is hard for those who trust in riches to enter the kingdom of God—He was saying it is *impossible.* That's why the disciples were shocked and wondered if anyone could be saved. In fact, Jesus specifically said it was impossible: "Jesus looking upon them saith, With men it is impossible, but not with God: for with God all things are possible" (Mark 10:27).

The point is that you can't sidestep the issue of trusting God with your finances. This is square one. Trusting God with your finances, as we've seen, is the least use of your faith, and if you aren't faithful in that which is least, then you won't be faithful in greater things. In my own life, I couldn't be doing the things I am doing now if I hadn't started with trusting God in my finances.

> *Once you begin trusting God for that which is seen—money—then you will be able to trust Him for that which is unseen: health, peace, joy, prosperity, and God's favor in your life.*

God has a plan for every Christian, and His plans are bigger than our dreams (Jeremiah 29:11; 1 Corinthians 2:9). I don't think anyone has maxed out God's plans for them. God will do great things, but you have to rely on Him. One of the first steps in that direction is becoming a faithful steward of God's resources. Once you begin trusting God for that which is seen—money—then you will be able to trust Him for that which is unseen: health, peace, joy, prosperity, and God's favor in your life.

I've mentioned the parable of the unjust steward a few times, but now I want to take a closer look at what Jesus was teaching. This parable is one of Jesus' hardest teachings to understand. You have to have a pretty good revelation on prosperity before you can decipher what the Lord is talking about here. I think understanding this parable will make a big difference in the way you view and use money. The parable starts like this:

> *[Jesus] said also unto his disciples, There was a certain rich man, which had a steward; and the same was accused unto him that he had wasted his goods. And he called him, and said unto him, How is it that I hear this of thee? give an account of thy stewardship; for thou mayest be no longer steward.*
>
> *Luke 16:1–2*

This parable tells of a wealthy man who had someone managing his money. The wealthy man thought that the steward was stealing from him, or somehow mismanaging his funds, so he told the steward to get his books in order: "Then the steward said within himself, What shall I do? for my lord taketh away from me the stewardship: I cannot dig; to beg I am ashamed" (Luke 16:3).

You can tell from the steward's reaction that he was guilty. He didn't try to prove his innocence or defend himself in any way. He knew that when his master took a look at the books, he was going to get fired. It was basically an admission of guilt. So the steward said, "What am I going to do? I can't dig." It's probably not true that he couldn't dig. It is probably more accurate to say he *wouldn't* dig.

This raises a good point: not everyone who has financial problems is lazy, but lazy people usually have financial problems. They're looking for a quick fix. They're looking to win the lottery or something. That's not how God's system works. If you are looking to prosper through winning the lottery, then you have the wrong attitude toward finances. The lottery isn't sinful necessarily, but it is a compromise. Expecting to get rich quick is never God's system of prosperity. Even if you were to defy the odds and strike it rich, Scripture says that wealth obtained through vanity doesn't last (Proverbs 13:11). Prosperity isn't about getting money any way you can—there is a right and a wrong way to do it.

I'm sure the steward could have found a job if he wanted to, but that isn't the way he thought. He didn't want to work to get his money. He wanted to steal it, inherit it, or come by it effortlessly somehow. He was always looking for some scheme instead of simply believing that God would bless his work. After concluding that he didn't want to look for work, he said, "I am ashamed to beg." It's too bad he wasn't ashamed to steal—he might still have a job! Having ruled out working and begging, the steward struck upon a scheme he liked.

> *I am resolved what to do, that, when I am put out of the stewardship, they may receive me into their houses. So he called every one of his lord's debtors unto him, and said unto the first, How much owest thou unto my lord? And he said, An hundred measures of oil. And he said unto him, Take thy bill, and sit down quickly, and write fifty. Then said*

he to another, And how much owest thou? And he said, An
hundred measures of wheat. And he said unto him, Take thy
bill, and write fourscore.

Luke 16:4–7

The parable only lists two debtors, but I believe those were simply given as examples of what the steward did. The wealthy man wouldn't have needed a steward to run his finances if only two people owed him money, so I'm sure many people were indebted to him. These examples show that the steward called in all of his master's debtors and cut their debt by huge margins. He gave them all discounts. He was too lazy to work and too proud to beg, so he kept on stealing money—but instead of putting the money into his own pocket, he put the money in the pockets of people who owed his master money.

I don't know how much a hundred measures of oil was worth, but I'm sure it was a lot of money. The steward probably cut this man's debt by the equivalent of tens of thousands of dollars today, and he did that for all of his master's debtors, which means there could have been dozens or even hundreds of people who saved thousands of dollars because of the steward's discounts. The logic behind this was that when the steward got fired he could go back to all of those debtors and say, "Hey, remember how I saved you thousands of dollars? Well, I'm out of work now. Can you give me a hand?" All of those people would feel indebted to him, or responsible for his unemployment, and he could "mooch" off of them instead of getting a job.

Up until this point, the parable isn't difficult to understand; it's about a man who didn't use his master's money properly and was going to be fired for it. We don't know if he was actually stealing or if he was just a bad steward, but either way, he was going to get fired. So he essentially used his master's money to bribe other people. He used his master's money to influence people and win favors. People steal money from their employers all of the time, so there isn't anything we've read so far that is all that strange. What's unusual about this story is the master's response: "The lord commended the unjust steward, because he had done wisely: for the children of this world are in their generation wiser than the children of light" (Luke 16:8).

The simple fact that the master found something to commend the steward on says a lot about the master's attitude toward money. Think about it, would you pay compliments to someone you caught stealing from you? If you came home one night and discovered a thief standing in your living room with a pillowcase stuffed full of your valuables, would you say to him, "Wow, you're doing a great job!" Would you compliment the thief for bypassing your security system and nabbing your most valuable goods?

The master's reaction to catching a thief is not what you'd expect. He didn't get angry or demand justice. He actually complimented the steward. It's possible that the master was so filthy rich that he didn't care if people stole from him, but I doubt it. If he didn't care about his money, he wouldn't have called the steward to account in the first place. I think this master understood that money is just a tool. It's not what we are meant to value. The blessing and favor of God are what makes us rich—not money.

I believe the master knew that money isn't the important part of prosperity. Most people judge their worth by their savings and retirement fund, but those things are just a physical manifestation of the real asset—which is God's favor. Wealth is just a by-product of God's favor. The Lord told Abraham, "I will bless thee, and make thy name great; and thou shalt be a blessing" (Genesis 12:2). It was the spoken favor of God on Abraham's life that caused him to prosper. It was God's favor that allowed him to grow rich from grazing his cattle and sheep in a desert. So it was in Jesus' parable. The master obviously had a revelation that his true wealth was the favor of God, not the money the steward was stealing.

The blessing and favor of God are what make you rich—not money.

This goes back to the first point I made about being a steward and recognizing that everything we have comes from God. God gives us resources, but the resources aren't our real asset. It's like the old children's fable about the goose that lays golden eggs. The golden eggs are not as valuable as the goose that produces them! The goose lays a golden egg every day, and when you have the goose, you get all of the golden eggs that come with it. In the same way, money isn't your true asset. The real treasure is the blessing and the favor of God that produces riches.

A lot of people today are focused on gathering golden eggs, and they are completely overlooking the parent force that creates them. The person who owns the goose is going to end up with a lot more gold than someone who is running around looking for eggs. Likewise, once you realize that God is the source of prosperity, you understand how pointless it is to chase after riches. This is one reason why Scripture reminds us that the power to get wealth comes from God.

> *Thou shalt remember the* LORD *thy God: for it is he that giveth thee power to get wealth, that he may establish his covenant which he sware unto thy fathers, as it is this day.*

> *Deuteronomy 8:18*

God is the source of our prosperity, but notice the scripture doesn't say God gives us wealth. God doesn't send us checks in the mail; He gives us the power to get wealth. He releases an anointing on whatever you do and causes it to prosper—and the blessing of God is so powerful that it cannot be reversed. Balaam is the infamous prophet who was hired by a foreign king to curse the children of Israel, but he said, "Behold, I have received commandment to bless: and [God] hath blessed; and I cannot reverse it" (Numbers 23:20).

Once the favor of God is on our lives, it cannot be stopped! The only thing that can derail the blessing of God is our own unbelief and negativity. As long as we keep believing, the blessings of God will keep coming. Understanding the true value of God's favor on your life will cause you to have the same attitude that the rich master had toward his steward in Luke 16. You can look at all of the things you possess and say, "It's just stuff." You'll know that money is merely a tool that helps you accomplish what God has called you to do—it isn't true prosperity.

Riches can be stolen and property can be taken away, but no one can rob you of God's favor. The rich master knew where his real treasure was, and that is why he didn't get angry with the steward.

He wasn't counting his paper money or coins as his true net worth. Once you get that same mindset, you can catch a thief robbing you blind and not feel fear or panic. You can get to where your life isn't bound up in things. You can become so secure in your relationship with God, and so certain of His favor in your life, that you actually find something to compliment a thief about.

The wealth you amass in life isn't important. The focus of your life should be your relationship with God, which is what causes wealth to accumulate. Money isn't that significant. On the other hand, God's favor in your life is priceless.

A good friend of mine, Pastor Bob Nichols, pastors Calvary Cathedral in Fort Worth, Texas. In April 2000, a tornado hit the area and destroyed his church. It was an $18 million facility, not including the building's contents, and in less than sixty seconds it was completely obliterated. Within one hour of the storm, CNN was standing in front of the wreckage interviewing Pastor Bob. He had his hard hat on, and he was saying, "God didn't do this. This is nothing but an attack of the devil." He said God was going to work it together for good, and they were going to end up with a facility twice as nice as the one that was destroyed.

Pastor Bob was expressing the same attitude that the rich master had. He could see all of his physical assets were destroyed, but it didn't shake his faith because his faith wasn't in physical assets. He knew that the blessing of God was what produced all of those things, and he still had God's favor. The storm had taken his property, but God's blessing was still on his life. Eventually Pastor Bob did end up with a facility twice as nice as the one destroyed by the tornado. His confidence was in the Lord, and the Lord restored everything that was taken from him—and then some.

This is exactly the way the rich master was thinking. He found an employee stealing what could have been millions of dollars from him, and it didn't faze him one bit. People on Wall Street start jumping out of windows when they lose millions because all of their trust and confidence is in money. Financial crisis pushes a lot of people over the edge, but—like the rich master—you won't be shaken if your trust is in the Lord.

You can only have that kind of confidence when you quit basing your life on physical things, and rely on God. When your trust is in what money can do for you, then your security is in your bank account—and when your bank account gets low, you are going to feel frightened and insecure. But when you know God is your source, you won't cling to assets. This mindset will help you sleep at night! It will completely transform your life to learn to rely on God instead of trusting in assets or other people. You can actually live your life without being tied to, or a servant of, your money. Money is nothing! It's the blessing and the favor of God on you that is the real asset.

The true power of money is in using it to change your future.

The other important point to understand from the parable of the unjust steward is why the steward's master commended him. You wouldn't think there is anything commendable about stealing money and giving it to other people, yet Jesus tells us that the master praised the steward for stealing. Here's the reason the rich master was commending the steward: the steward finally realized that the true power of money is in using it to affect the future. Instead of pocketing the stolen money, the steward was using it to bribe people and prepare for his future.

It's easy to see that prior to this, the steward must have been frivolously spending the money on things—he was buying fancy cars, caviar, flat-screen TVs, nice clothes, jewelry, and things like that. He obviously didn't have any money saved, because he thought he was going to have to dig ditches or beg (Luke 16:3).

The master wasn't commending the steward for the act of stealing—he was complimenting the steward for finally figuring out that money is a tool. It doesn't matter what country you live in or how much money you have in the bank. Most people make the critical mistake of using money only for temporary short-term things. They spend their money on things that give a little bit of momentary reward, and they ignore the power money has to shape their future.

To a degree, lost people are better stewards of their assets than Christians are; that's not always the case, but often it is. I believe this is what Jesus was getting at when He said, "The children of this world are in their generation wiser than the children of light" (Luke 16:8). Part of the reason is that Christians know this life isn't all there is. Lost people are planning for retirement and thinking death is the end, whereas Christians aren't as short term in their thinking.

Most Christians don't have the same fear of death that unbelievers have, and we look beyond this life into eternity. As a result, a lot of Christians don't prepare for their later years in life or gather an inheritance to leave for their children. But money doesn't just give you power to shape your future on earth—it also influences eternity. When Jesus was done teaching about the rich master who commended the unjust steward, He said:

> *I say unto you, Make to yourselves friends of the mammon of unrighteousness; that, when ye fail, they may receive you into everlasting habitations.*

Luke 16:9

The Greek word translated as "fail" here also means death or "die."[9] This scripture is telling us to use money ("the mammon of unrighteousness"[10]) to make friends who will receive us into everlasting habitations when we die. In other words, you can touch people's lives through giving, and when you die, those people will be lined up in heaven to thank you for the way you used your resources to help them. You can do it by giving to people directly or by giving to support the preaching of the Gospel, which saves, heals, and delivers.

Money is only temporary. It doesn't exist in heaven, and you can't take it with you when you die—that's why you'll never see a hearse pulling a moving van. Paper money, gold, coins, diamonds, and silver are all temporary; one day, they will all be burned up (2 Peter 3:10). But by investing money in the lives of others, you

---

[9] Adam Clarke, *Adam Clarke's Commentary on the Bible,* available from http://studylight.org/com/acc/view.cgi?book=lu&chapter=016, S.V. "When ye fail," Luke 16:9.
[10] *The People's New Testament*, available from http://www.biblestudytools.com/commentaries/peoples-new-testament, S.V., "9. Mammon of Unrighteousness," Luke 16:9.

can take something that is destined for destruction and turn it into something eternal. You can transform money into something that will never pass away by investing it in the Gospel and by using it to touch other people's lives.

The purpose of this parable is to show us that the best use of money isn't on temporary things that are going to pass away. Prosperity isn't about your house or car. It's not about having the latest gadgets and the fanciest clothes. The number one use of your money is to touch people's lives.

Every natural thing that you have used your money to purchase is going to be destroyed one day. It doesn't matter how much you have in this life. Some of the people who are greatly admired now because of all of their wealth aren't going to have a single person waiting in heaven to thank them for using their money to change lives. A lot of people who have put their trust in money won't even make it to heaven, but I also believe there are Christians who won't have much treasure waiting in heaven. They'll still be blessed and overwhelmed by the love of God because we aren't saved according to our works, but there won't be anybody waiting to welcome them into heaven because they never used their money to spread the Gospel and change lives.

Other people who were not highly esteemed in this life will have people lined up by the thousands waiting to welcome them. They might not have lived in the nicest house on the block, but they will have given from their resources to bless others, and their giving will have transformed into eternal treasure. You won't know how many lives you have touched by giving to support the preaching of the Gospel until you get to heaven and see everyone lined up to greet you.

Yes, God wants you to take care of your needs. You aren't a good steward if your family is sleeping under a tree because you keep giving all of your money away. God wants you to live in comfort, dress well, and own nice things. He doesn't want you to be poor. God is not against you taking care of yourself. What I'm saying is that your attitude about money will change when you really get a revelation on prosperity. You'll be thinking, *How little money do I need to take care of my family, and how much can I invest in eternity?*

A million years from now, people will still be stopping by your mansion in glory to thank you for the investment you made in the Gospel and for the way it touched their lives. No saint will be saying, "Oh, I sure wish I'd spent my money on a nicer car or a third flat-screen television." No way.

> *A man is not a fool to give away something he can't keep in order to get something he can never lose.*

God is in the people business! All material things are going to fade away, and the only thing that will matter is how much you invested in people. One day, you will be thankful that you got money out of your pocket and put it into the Gospel. Everything you hold on to, you end up losing. It's only what you give away that you get to keep, and no one is a fool to give away something they can't keep in order to get something they can never lose.

When the master told the steward he was going to be fired, the steward finally got the message that he had better start planning for the future. He realized that he needed to take the money he had access to and use the influence and power it gave him to prepare his future. Jesus used that parable to teach us that the best use of money is not to buy things, but to touch lives and change people.

Unfortunately, I don't think many people have understood or embraced the mind-set Jesus was teaching through this parable. Most people take care of themselves first, and tip God from the remains. After every lust and desire of their heart has been satisfied, they give God the leftovers. God isn't mad at them, but they are missing the benefits of good financial stewardship. It is far better to learn to live on less money, and to use a portion of our resources to affect the future.

I'm not saying you are supposed to keep your nose to the grindstone and not enjoy the journey of life. You need to keep a balance between planning for the future and living in the moment, but—at least in the United States—a lot of people have swung clear over to gratifying every whim and thinking only about the moment. People are mortgaging their future so they can enjoy everything right now. They are indulging themselves by grabbing everything they can, and they aren't planning for the future at all. Like the unjust steward, they would do well to recognize that money is best spent on the future.

The two main points we learn from the parable of the dishonest steward are that money is not our greatest asset, and wise people invest their money in the future. Remember, the blessing of God is what makes you rich, not money. As long as you have God's blessing, wealth will find you. The key is learning not to spend all of your money on short-lived pleasures, but using some of it to help shape your future. Not just on earth, but so multitudes of people will be waiting to welcome you into heaven.

Chapter 5

Seek First the Kingdom

I t's important to have the right attitude about finances before you start focusing on God's desire to bring money your way. Scripture says that if your eye is single then your whole body will be flooded with light, but if your eye is evil then your body is full of darkness (Matthew 6:22–23). It also says that anyone who hastens to be rich has an evil eye (Proverbs 28:22). In other words, if your focus is divided between the things of God and getting rich, then your whole body will be full of darkness.

This is a very important concept. The Lord is saying that He wants you to be single in your focus upon Him. At first, you might think it is impossible to be totally committed to and focused upon God in everything you do, and if we had to rely on human strength, I would agree. But we don't live the Christian life in our own strength. The apostle Paul wrote,

> *(For the weapons of our warfare are not carnal, but mighty through God to the pulling down of strong holds;) Casting down imaginations, and every high thing that exalteth itself against the knowledge of God, and bringing into captivity every thought to the obedience of Christ.*
>
> *2 Corinthians 10:4–5*

God has given us weapons so strong that they can bring every thought into obedience to Christ. You can work, raise a family, do all of the things you need to do in life, and still keep your attention 100 percent upon God. *But you can't be focused on God when you think you are the one who is responsible for producing the financial blessing in your life!* If you think that supporting your family and earning money is strictly up to you, then you are going to have a divided heart—and a divided heart is going to allow darkness to enter your life and hinder you in your relationship with God.

The apostle Paul also said, "This one thing I do" (Philippians 3:13). The reason he accomplished everything he did was because he did one thing: he sought first the kingdom of God. The quickest way to destroy a person's vision is to give him or her two. You can't accomplish your goals when your attention and resources are divided. If you really want to prosper, then you need to forget everything else and press toward this one goal of putting the kingdom first.

I know you might be thinking, *You're living in la-la land. Out in the real world, you have to work to pay bills. Life is all about working to get ahead.* It's true that we are supposed to work. Scripture says that lazy people who don't work shouldn't expect to eat, but God's plan for our financial freedom doesn't rely on the natural results of hard work (2 Thessalonians 3:10). We have to change the way we think about money and prosperity. Paul encouraged the Ephesians to think differently about the goal of work when he said, "Let him that stole steal no more: but rather let him labour, working with his hands the thing which is good, that he may have to give to him that needeth" (Ephesians 4:28).

He didn't tell them to labor so they could pay their bills and keep a roof over their heads. Nor did he tell them to labor so they could feed and clothe their children. He said, "work so you'll have money to give to those in need." He was echoing Jesus' teaching that the most important use of money is not satisfying temporary needs. By satisfying other people's temporal needs, Paul was saying, they could demonstrate the love of God and touch people's lives.

Every dollar you get has the potential to influence a person's life for the better. Of course, you have needs too, and God knows that. The natural inclination is to think, *If I start taking care of everybody else, then who is going to take care of me?* God! God will take care of you, and He'll do a better job than you ever have. This is where you see that finances are a matter of faith. You can't dissect what I'm saying and see exactly how it works. I can't write out a contract and say that if you do these things, you are going to have more money than you ever dreamed.

Prosperity is a by-product of seeking God; it shouldn't be the goal.

But the Word teaches that when you put the kingdom of God first, then all of your financial needs will be taken care of (Matthew 6:33). Prosperity is a by-product of seeking God; it shouldn't be the goal.

What I'm talking about here is a matter of the heart. You can't create some kind of formula from what I'm saying where you put effort in on one end and prosperity comes out the other. God's financial system doesn't work the same way that the world's system works. God's kind of prosperity results from faith. When you work so that you can have money to give, God takes care of you. It's a mindset and a heart condition, not a get-rich-quick scheme.

God's kind of prosperity comes when you shift your focus from getting and maintaining stuff to living to give. Most people say, "I want to give...and if I ever get any extra, I will." We saw earlier that what they mean is that as soon as they get everything they want, they'll toss a tip God's way. As long as their needs get met first, then God can have the leftovers; that isn't seeking first the kingdom of God. The Lord says we should work so we will have money to bless other people.

The highest form of giving is to help share the Gospel. When you start helping the Good News to be shared, demonstrating the love of God in word and deed, there is a divine flow that takes place. God starts supernaturally supplying your needs. This is why Scripture tells us to give God the firstfruits—not the leftover fruit. The first thing you should do when you get money is give back to God. When you do that, God takes better care of you accidentally than you have ever done through striving and grasping at your resources.

The reason some Christians preach about financial prosperity and believe for it so hard is that they want the new houses, cars, and things they see people in the world enjoying. They are preaching about prosperity, but it's all about them. They wear huge jewelry and flash their money around just like unbelievers. Again, there's nothing wrong with being prosperous. God wants you to have nice things, but your heart attitude should be that prosperity isn't about you—it's really about how much is flowing through you.

God gave us two hands: one hand to receive and one hand to give. If God can get the money through you to other people, then He will get it to you—and as the money flows through there will be plenty leftover for you. You are not supposed to live in poverty; it's just that your first priority should be helping other people, rather than trying to grab everything you can for yourself.

It's the same attitude we are taught in Scripture: "God is able to make all grace abound toward you; that ye, always having all sufficiency in all things, may abound to every good work" (2 Corinthians 9:8). The context of this scripture is money. The apostle Paul was writing to the Corinthians about being good stewards. It's not just about spiritual blessings. This is saying that the reason God makes all financial blessings abound toward you is so that you'll have the resources to do good things for others—because true prosperity isn't defined by how nice your house is or by

Prosperity isn't about you—it's really about how much money is flowing through you.

what kind of car you drive. God evaluates prosperity by how much of a blessing you are to others. This is all easy to say, but it's a lot harder to live.

The average high school graduate in the United States earns more than one million dollars in their lifetime, and college graduates earn twice that. Many people will have had one or two million dollars pass through their hands in this life, but they won't have anything to show for it in eternity. They will have spent all of their money on cars, clothes, and food. Right now, we have the privilege of taking something that will eventually be completely destroyed and converting it into something that will never pass away. Once you understand this truth, you realize what an incredible blessing it is to be able to give. It's the investment opportunity of a lifetime.

My wife and I had virtually nothing when we started out in ministry. We've been through a lot of hard financial times. Most of it was because of the religious bondage and wrong doctrine I believed that was keeping me from experiencing God's blessing, but we always put God first, and God has blessed us as a result. We put our focus on seeking God and giving to others, and the side effect for us has been prosperity—that's how God's financial system works.

The carnal mind thinks, *If I don't take care of myself, no one else will either,* and I guess that's true if you don't have faith in God. But when you trust God and begin honoring Him with your firstfruits, then God will make your "barns be filled with plenty, and thy presses...burst out with new wine" (Proverbs 3:10). He causes a supernatural flow of finances toward you. God's promise is this: "Seek ye first the kingdom of God, and his righteousness; and all these things shall be added unto you" (Matthew 6:33).

What "things" will be added unto you? In context, Jesus was talking about where you sleep, what you eat, and the clothes you wear. He was saying that finances will be added unto you. So when you put the kingdom of God first, God takes care of your physical needs. In other words, when your first priority is seeking God, then He assumes the responsibility of taking care of you—and God will do a lot better job than you can.

In the Old Testament, Elijah prophesied to King Ahab that a drought was coming, and then he fled into the desert to hide. King Ahab was persecuting God's prophets, so Elijah had to run for his life. Initially, God sent ravens to feed him at a brook. When the brook dried up, God told Elijah to go to the city of Zarephath where He had commanded a widow to sustain him. So Elijah went to the city and found the widow woman. The first thing he said to her was, "Go get me some water, and while you're at it, bring me something to eat" (1 Kings 17:10–11). The widow turned to him and said,

> *As the LORD thy God liveth, I have not a cake, but an*
> *handful of meal in a barrel, and a little oil in a cruse: and,*
> *behold, I am gathering two sticks, that I may go in and dress*
> *it for me and my son, that we may eat it, and die.*
>
> *1 Kings 17:12*

Water is obviously a precious commodity during a drought, yet the widow was still willing to go get Elijah some water. But she drew a line when he asked for food. This widow was down to her very last meal. She and her son were going to die of starvation after they ate it because they had absolutely nothing left. Elijah told her to go make his meal first and bring it to him. Then, he said, she could go cook for herself and her son, and he told her what would happen if she did as he requested.

> *For thus saith the LORD God of Israel, The barrel of meal*
> *shall not waste, neither shall the cruse of oil fail, until the day*
> *that the LORD sendeth rain upon the earth.*
>
> *1 Kings 17:14*

The widow only had enough oil and flour for one tiny meal, but she believed what Elijah told her so she made his meal first. As a result, the Lord supernaturally maintained the tiny amount of oil and flour in her containers and it fed Elijah, the widow, and her son for three years. Can you imagine what bystanders would have thought if they had heard Elijah telling a widow to give him her last meal? They would have accused him of stealing from her. The *Jerusalem Post* headline would have been, "Man of God Takes Widow's Last Meal." But Elijah wasn't taking from the widow—he was giving to her.

If the widow hadn't given him that meal, then the Lord wouldn't have supernaturally multiplied the food, and the widow and her son would have died of starvation within days. The step of faith she took by feeding God's prophet first, before taking care of herself, resulted in a supply that supported her and her son for three years. Later on, Elijah also raised her son from the dead (vv. 17–24), which wouldn't have happened if she hadn't formed a relationship with Elijah through feeding him for three years. So her giving of the little bit she had was the way to multiple miracles in her life.

I remember ministering on these same passages years ago at a church in Texas. At the end of the service, a woman came up to me asking for prayer. She asked me if I remembered who she was, and I said no. She went on to tell me how I had prayed for her the year before. At the time, she was living in a mental institution and wanted God to restore her mind. I prayed for her, and she had been completely healed—praise God! She was eventually released from the institution, but she didn't have anywhere to go, so the institution gave her a place to live and a job as a custodian. But she wanted to be totally free from that place, and to do that, she needed a financial miracle. She needed a new job and a new place to live.

Well, I had just finished preaching about Elijah telling the widow to give to him first and how the widow's step of faith opened up God's supernatural provision. So I told the woman that she needed to give. "What do you have?" I asked.

She got her purse and took out a little coin pouch. She emptied the coin pouch into my hand, and it was something like $87 and change.

"Give it to me," I said.

"All of it?" she asked.

"All of it," I said.

She gave me every last penny. She said she wouldn't have any money until she got paid again, and she hadn't even bought groceries yet. To top it off, it was going to be more than a week until her next payday. But I took all of her money and gave it to the pastor of the church, and then I prayed for her financial miracle.

That pastor called me the next week to tell me what had happened. The Monday after we prayed, someone who didn't even go to their church gave the woman a car. It wasn't anyone who knew that she needed a car. It was just God's supernatural provision. A day or two after that, the woman's mother called. Previously, her mother had been embarrassed by her condition and severed all relations with her when she entered the mental institution. The mother asked forgiveness for the way she had treated her and asked her to move back home. By the end of the week, the woman had a new job that paid twice as much.

> *God assumes the responsibility of taking care of you when you put seeking His kingdom first. And God can take far better care of you than you can.*

Someone who didn't have faith in God might have thought I was being cruel to ask for that woman's last penny, but I wasn't taking from her. I was giving her an opportunity to activate God's supernatural flow, and her step of faith got her a car, a place to live, a restored relationship with her mother, and a new job that paid twice what her old job did! That's awesome. It shows God's concern for every aspect of our lives. He wants us to prosper in every way: physically, emotionally, financially, and in our relationships. When we put the kingdom of God first, God takes care of our needs supernaturally. So if you want God to assume all of your financial liabilities, then put the kingdom of God first in your finances.

This might seem like a radical concept, but it works. It has worked in my life, and I've seen it work in the lives of hundreds of others. You are going to wind up frustrated if you think that work is all about getting money so that you can pay your bills. It's discouraging to get up every morning and go to work just so you can make your house payment and buy food and clothes. There is a better way to live!

> *Lay not up for yourselves treasures upon earth, where moth and rust doth corrupt, and where thieves break through and steal.*

> *Matthew 6:19*

It would be a mistake to interpret this verse to mean that you can't ever have any money. Another scripture tells us we should leave an inheritance for our children's children, and you need to save up quite a bit of money to do that (Proverbs 13:22). I think what Jesus is getting at here is our motives. It's wrong to build up savings out of fear, or so that you can sit back and say to yourself, "Eat, drink, and be merry, for I have goods laid up for many days ahead" (Luke 12:19). That's the wrong attitude. But it's good to build up savings so that you always have resources to "abound to every good work" (2 Corinthians 9:8), and to leave an inheritance to your grandchildren. That's using money to bless others.

When Jesus said these things, no doubt He knew people would be asking, "How do you seek first the kingdom of God and build up an inheritance at the same time? If I do everything for the sake of the Lord, who is going to pay my rent, buy my clothes, and provide food for me to eat?" So Jesus said,

> *No man can serve two masters: for either he will hate the one, and love the other; or else he will hold to the one, and despise the other. Ye cannot serve God and mammon. Therefore I say unto you, Take no thought for your life, what ye shall eat, or what ye shall drink; nor yet for your body, what ye shall put on. Is not the life more than meat, and the body than raiment?*
>
> *Matthew 6:24–25*

This clearly says that we can't serve God and money, but that doesn't mean you'll never have money when you serve God. It's obvious that we should choose to serve God, so Jesus goes on to explain how God takes care of our needs. Life, He tells us, is about more than eating and deciding which clothes to wear. Besides, worrying about your finances won't help anyway.

> *Behold the fowls of the air: for they sow not, neither do they reap, nor gather into barns; yet your heavenly Father feedeth them. Are ye not much better than they? Which of you by taking thought can add one cubit unto his stature?*
>
> *Matthew 6:26–27*

Have you ever read a headline about millions of birds dying of starvation? No. And you never will. They don't plant, or harvest, or store food away—yet God feeds them. If God cares that much for a tiny little bird, think how much better care He will take of a person who has been made in His image (Genesis 1:26)! Jesus is encouraging us that we can have much more confidence in God to take care of us. This is a radical statement. We seem to feel like it's our duty to worry about things, but God is telling us to rely on Him with our whole heart (Proverbs 3:5; 1 Peter 5:7).

> *Therefore take no thought, saying, What shall we eat? or, What shall we drink? or, Wherewithal shall we be clothed? (For after all these things do the Gentiles seek:) for your heavenly Father knoweth that ye have need of all these things.*
>
> *Matthew 6:31–32*

In modern language, we'd say that those are things lost people seek after (v. 32). There should be a difference between Christians and unbelievers—between people who have a covenant with God, and people who are trying to do it all on their own. The world should be able to see a difference in every area of our lives, including finances. We shouldn't be out in the world chasing money and struggling to survive the same way that unbelievers are. God wants us to prosper, and we have a covenant that includes financial prosperity. God is pleased when you prosper! He wants to see you succeed. (See Psalm 35:27 and 3 John 2, for example.)

After giving us all of this reassurance, Jesus tells us to seek first the kingdom of God and "all of these things shall be added unto you." What things? The same things He was talking about earlier: what you eat, where you sleep, the clothes you wear, and all of your physical needs. Remember, when you put the kingdom of God first, God takes care of everything else.

Many of us work our fingers to the bone trying to get ahead. We have garage sales; we scrimp and save or work two jobs. We get a more fuel-efficient car. We do anything we can to save a little money. But all of that is really about meeting our own needs and taking care of our responsibilities. At the end of the day, if we have any spare money lying around, then we give to God to promote the Gospel.

The scriptural way to live is to seek first the kingdom of God— even with our finances (Matthew 6:33). We should be working to give. When your heart is transformed and you start working so that you can be a blessing to other people, then God starts taking better care of you than you ever took of yourself. God is El Shaddai, not El Cheapo. When you seek first the kingdom of God, even in your giving and finances, then God prospers you.

This is a truth you need to open up your heart to and allow the Holy Spirit to reveal. I can explain it, but it's going to take a supernatural revelation to really get what I'm talking about here. You can't just go through the motions of giving and think that God is going to return your giving one hundred times over. You have to rely on God and trust that He is your source. It has to be a heart-level revelation, not just a conclusion you arrive at mentally. But once you grab hold of this, it will revolutionize your life. You will be completely transformed once you believe that by putting God first, He will begin to supernaturally take care of you. It will bring you a tremendous amount of peace and confidence.

Chapter 6

Prosperity Isn't Selfish

The book of Matthew gives a lengthy description of stewardship in its final chapters. It starts in Chapter 25 with the story of ten virgins, some of whom didn't manage the oil in their lamps well (vv. 1–12). Then, in that same chapter, we are given the parable about three servants who were entrusted with money by their master. The master gave one servant five talents, another two talents, and the last servant one talent. (A talent was a specific weight of money in coins.[11]) The servant with five talents took what his master had given him and made another five talents. Likewise, the servant with two talents made an additional two talents. But the man who received one talent just buried it for safekeeping.

Later, the master returned and asked the servants what they had done with his money. The servant who made five talents was commended by the master, and so was the servant who made two talents. When the servant who received one talent came before the master he said,

---

[11] Thayer and Smith, "Greek Lexicon entry for Talanton," available from http://www.biblestudytools.com/lexicons/greek/kjv/talanton.html, Strong's #5007, S.V. "talent," Matthew 25:15.

Lord, I knew thee that thou art an hard man, reaping where thou hast not sown, and gathering where thou hast not strawed: And I was afraid, and went and hid thy talent in the earth.

Matthew 25:24–25

Then he gave back the one talent he had received. The master was furious. He rebuked the servant for not having at least put the money in the bank to earn interest, and then he said,

Take therefore the talent from him, and give it unto him which hath ten talents. For unto every one that hath shall be given, and he shall have abundance: but from him that hath not shall be taken away even that which he hath. And cast ye the unprofitable servant into outer darkness: there shall be weeping and gnashing of teeth.

Matthew 25:28–30

This passage says that because the poorer servant didn't invest what he was given, even the little he had was taken away, and he was cast into outer darkness. It clearly reveals that the Lord expects us to take what He has given us and do something with it, not just hide it in the earth. Our God is a God of multiplication. He wants us to increase the resources we are given, not just spend our money on carnal appetites.

Right after giving this parable, Jesus talks about coming back in glory and separating the sheep from the goats (vv. 31–33). To some He will say, "Come, ye blessed of my Father, inherit the kingdom prepared for you from the foundation of the world" (v. 34). Those are the people who clothed the naked, fed the sick, gave water to the thirsty, and visited inmates in prison (vv. 35–36). This is all still related to stewardship. Jesus is talking about taking the resources God has blessed us with and using them to touch others. It takes money to visit people in prison. If nothing else, it's going to cost you gas and transportation. All ministry costs money.

Jesus said that those who never clothe the naked, care for the sick, or feed the hungry don't really know Him, and they will be cast into everlasting fire (vv. 41–46). Those are some strong words, and a lot of people don't like to hear them because it makes stewardship an integral part of what God expects us all to do. Many people aren't willing to give up control of their finances like that. In fact, the word *talent* in those verses is spiritualized by some who say it is talking about the spiritual gifts we have been given. I'm not saying you can't make that application, but Jesus was literally talking about money, which again shows that stewardship is far more important than it is typically given credit for being.

> *The motive behind what you do is more important than the action itself.*

Another problem some people have is thinking that prosperity is selfish. I've had lots of people tell me they are satisfied with what they have, and they don't want any more. I agree that being content with what you have is godly, but it's also selfish to say you don't want more resources. What most of those people are really saying is, "As long as my needs are met, then I'm satisfied. I don't need any more." What about everyone else? When you have excess money, you can be a blessing to those in need. Without extra finances, you are limited in your ability to give. It's better to prosper and increase your finances—not for yourself, but so you can be a blessing to someone else.

Prosperity isn't all about you. God entrusts us with resources so that we can be a blessing to other people, so it isn't selfish to desire prosperity. When you see God as your source and treat the money He gives you as a resource to be stewarded, then it is very godly to want to prosper so that you can give and help establish God's covenant on Earth.

On the other hand, you have people teaching prosperity from a selfish standpoint. Some preachers present prosperity like it's all about getting more. It's selfish, and the driving motive for that kind of prosperity is covetousness. You aren't going to see a supernatural return on your giving when you do it with the wrong motive. It has to come from a humble heart that desires to bless other people. Since the motive behind what you do is more important than the action itself, giving with a wrong heart is of no benefit.

Scripture says, "Though I bestow all my goods to feed the poor, and though I give my body to be burned, and have not charity, it profiteth me nothing" (1 Corinthians 13:3). This says you can go so far as to make the ultimate sacrifice of laying down your life, but it will be of no benefit to you whatsoever if it isn't done out of a motivation of love. It will bless the person you sacrifice yourself for, but it isn't going to result in a supernatural return for you.

Likewise, going out and playing the role of a good steward isn't going to help you at all if you aren't doing it with the right motivation. If your only reason for giving is so that God will give back to you, it isn't going to work. Yes, God wants you to prosper—

but having faith in God's provision is different from lusting after money and hoping for a supernatural flow of finances. Faith works, but carnal appetites are going to profit you nothing.

Some Christians have the wrong attitude about prosperity. When you talk about God's desire for us to prosper through stewardship, immediately their greed and selfishness kicks in. They start thinking, *Man, here is Scriptural justification for me to get as much stuff as I can, then can all I get and sit on my can. This is awesome!* Not really. It's true that God wants you to increase, but the motive behind your actions is super important.

Having the right motivations behind financial stewardship doesn't come naturally. Our society is so focused on self-fulfillment and self-gratification that living for God is a totally foreign concept. It doesn't make sense to the natural mind. Think of how the apostle Paul reacted to slavery. In his day, slavery was a very common practice. Paul was probably the most influential man in the body of Christ at the time, and he was in a position to change how Christians behaved. If he had spoken out against the unjust practice of slavery, then he probably would have set tens of thousands of slaves free, but he didn't do that.

For instance, Paul wrote a letter to Philemon to talk about his slave, Onesimus, who had run away and escaped to Rome (Philemon 1:10–19). Once in Rome, Onesimus encountered Paul, who led him to the Lord and then told him to go back to his master and submit to his position as a slave! God doesn't approve of slavery, and Paul knew that. Paul was just saying that there is no difference between slave and free: slaves are free in Christ, and the free are slaves to Christ. When your total life is in Christ, you have so much victory and contentment in the Lord that it doesn't matter whether you are living free or as a slave.

We are more humanistic today than people were in Paul's time, so you might find this attitude hard to stomach. Our society is all about personal freedoms and self-interest. I'd say that freedom is nearly a god to some people. Yet, here Paul is telling people not to despise Christian slave masters. A lot of people today would get bitter and say that a Christian should treat a slave differently—in fact, he should set them all free—but Paul tells slaves to serve their Christian slave masters even harder because they are brothers. When Paul was finished talking about slaves submitting to their masters, he said:

> *If any man teach otherwise, and consent not to wholesome*
> *words, even the words of our Lord Jesus Christ, and to*
> *the doctrine which is according to godliness; He is proud,*
> *knowing nothing, but doting about questions and strifes of*
> *words, whereof cometh envy, strife, railings, evil surmisings,*
> *perverse disputings of men of corrupt minds, and destitute*
> *of the truth, supposing that gain is godliness: from such*
> *withdraw thyself.*

> *1 Timothy 6:3–5*

Paul's words are a reminder that personal freedom isn't everything. Life isn't supposed to be all about taking care of ourselves and seeking our own gain. Yet we have an entire generation in the United States that has been called the "Me Generation." Most people are living very self-centered lives. Everything is all about "me." The truth is, when you're all wrapped up in yourself, you make a very small package.

In the United States, a lot has been made of the sacrifices carried out by the men who fought in World War II. A relative of mine was a Marine who fought at Iwo Jima. He was in one of the first waves of soldiers in the amphibious assault. Before they invaded, he was told that the first few waves of soldiers would never make it. They were basically being used to draw all of the enemy fire and expend their ammunition, but they were willing to make that sacrifice so that the waves of soldiers behind them would have a chance to survive and win the fight. They believed in making a sacrifice to win the war. They were committed to principle more than to self-interest, and they realized there was something more important than their individual freedom or existence.

> *Prosperity is having enough so that you can abound unto every good work.*

Selfishness is the most prevalent attitude today. A lot of people are making their decisions based purely upon whatever is best for them. If something promotes their personal well-being, then it's good—if not, then it's bad. They don't have any reference larger than their own needs. That kind of attitude is going to affect how you handle your finances. Paul made that application when he was finished talking about slavery:

> *Godliness with contentment is great gain. For we brought nothing into this world, and it is certain we can carry*

nothing out. And having food and raiment let us be
therewith content. But they that will be rich fall into
temptation and a snare, and into many foolish and hurtful
lusts, which drown men in destruction and perdition. For the
love of money is the root of all evil: which while some coveted
after, they have erred from the faith, and pierced themselves
through with many sorrows. But thou, O man of God, flee
these things; and follow after righteousness, godliness, faith,
love, patience, meekness. Fight the good fight of faith.

1 Timothy 6:6–12

Some people have taken these verses to mean that money itself is evil, but the word "contentment" in this passage is talking about having your needs met. It isn't saying that a godly attitude means you can't have riches. You can have both if your motive is right. Loving God doesn't mean you have to be poor, and having money doesn't mean you are ungodly. For one thing, wealth is relative. Some of the people preaching that you can't have money and still be a servant of God are extremely wealthy by the rest of the world's standards. We are super rich compared to the people Paul wrote this passage to. We have conveniences they couldn't have dreamed of: running hot water, air conditioning, indoor plumbing, microwaves, automobiles, and homes fit for kings. We are living in a period of unparalleled prosperity.

This passage of Scripture isn't saying we can't have money. It says the *love of* money is the root of all evil—not money itself. Money isn't the problem; it's the attitude that people have toward money. It's putting your trust in money and finding your fulfillment in it. If you just put your trust in God, then He will give you money to accomplish His instructions and the call He has placed on your life. The problem comes when you love money and what it will produce more than you love God, and when you rely on it instead of looking to God as your source.

It's amazing to me how religion has perverted this scripture, and we have Christians promoting poverty in the name of the Lord. It isn't godly to be poor any more than it is godly to be rich. Money has nothing to do with godliness. God doesn't want us to always be dependent upon others because we are poor. He wants us to be able to help others out financially. He wants Christians to be part of the answer, not part of the problem, and to do that we have to have financial increase. I know a lot has been taught about money being evil, but if we want to be a blessing to others then we have to drop our prejudices against having money.

Now, this might sound strange. You may be thinking, *Who could have a prejudice against having money?* Well, I did! I was raised in a pretty affluent home compared to the other kids I grew up with, but I had been taught that it was ungodly for people who serve God to have money. I remember a missionary couple coming to speak at my church when I was young and instead of getting a hotel or something, they slept in the back of their station wagon. They didn't want to spend any money on a hotel. The wife only had two dresses—she washed one every night and wore the other the next day. I'm telling you, our pastor set that couple on a pedestal and promoted them as an ideal example of how true Christians should live. They were "suffering for Jesus."

I look back on that now and realize what a completely backward model of poverty that was. God doesn't want you sleeping in the back of your car or not having enough clothes to wear. What a terrible witness! It makes it look like God can't even take care of His own children.

Part of the cause for my financial problems when I first got started in ministry was that I was embarrassed to have things. I thought that ministers were supposed to do without. Have you ever seen someone go into a store and ask for a discount because they are a minister? I don't like seeing things like that; it's like announcing to the world that Christians can't compete or prosper. It's a kind of begging and telling the world that we need help. Yet Scripture says, "[I have never] seen the righteous forsaken, nor his seed begging bread" (Psalm 37:25). Poverty does not glorify God, and saying that it does is a perversion of Scripture.

Biblical prosperity isn't selfish, because it isn't about meeting personal needs. The Christian motivation for prosperity is about desiring to have the resources to bless others and accomplish what God has called you to do. Prosperity isn't about indulging your flesh; that's not it at all. Prosperity is about giving. When you get that attitude, God will get money to you—and there will be plenty leftover for you.

It's also important to remember that prosperity is relative. It isn't limited to those living in developed nations. Prosperity for a farmer in a small village might mean having ten goats instead of one. It might mean living in the nicest hut in your community and having six chickens instead of two. You don't have to live in a multimillion-dollar home in Beverly Hills in order to be prosperous. The standard of prosperity is relative, but these truths about prosperity will work in any situation, anywhere in the world. The key is having the right motivation and seeking God first. When you do that, you put yourself in a position to receive God's supernatural flow.

Scripture says, "God is able to make all grace abound toward you; that ye, always having all sufficiency in all things, may abound to every good work" (2 Corinthians 9:8). The reason God causes His grace to abound toward us is so that we will be able to abound unto every good work.

Remember, real prosperity is defined by how much we give away, not by how much we keep for ourselves. A lot of people look good on paper. They have a huge house, fancy things, and a ton of money in the stock market and all kinds of investments—but all of their money is tied up. I've had lots of "wealthy" people tell me that they'd like to give finances to our ministry, but they can't because they don't have any "liquid assets"; those people aren't really prosperous. If you are using all of your money for yourself, then you aren't prosperous. True prosperity is about giving and the ability to "abound to every good work." It isn't determined by the size of your house, by the car that you drive, or by jewels and expensive clothing. In fact, you can be prosperous without having any of those things.

The Old Testament tells the story of Joseph, who was sold into slavery as a young man. Slaves up for sale used to be stripped naked so that prospective buyers could see the physical condition of the slave they were buying. As Joseph was standing naked on an auction block, without a single possession to his name, the Bible says that he was a prosperous man (Genesis 39:1–2). See, prosperity isn't measured by how many assets you have. Joseph was a naked slave, but God was still with him, and it was just a matter of time before money started flowing his way.

God gives seed to sowers.

God's blessing on Joseph's life caused him to prosper in everything he did. Potiphar, the man who purchased Joseph as a slave, soon recognized the anointing on Joseph and put him in charge of his entire estate (v. 4). Potiphar's wife was even drawn to the anointing on Joseph, but when he refused to sleep with her, she lied about him and had him thrown in prison. But God was with Joseph even in prison. Before long, the head jailer turned the entire prison operation over to Joseph and let him run it (vv. 7–23).

While he was in prison, Joseph interpreted the dreams of two of Pharaoh's servants who had been confined with him. One servant was released and the other was executed, just as Joseph had interpreted (Genesis 40). Two years later, Pharaoh had a couple of dreams that no one could interpret for him and the released servant told Pharaoh about Joseph. Joseph was brought before Pharaoh, who said, "I hear you can interpret dreams."

"Not I," Joseph answered, "but God will interpret the dream for you." This reveals where Joseph's heart was: he always put God first. Sure enough, God interpreted the dream through Joseph, and Pharaoh made him second-in-command over all of Egypt. Joseph saved Egypt from famine, and he made Pharaoh even richer (Genesis 41).

Joseph prospered every life that he came into contact with. He was a super blessing. He helped other people, and eventually Joseph became rich himself, but it was never all about him. Joseph was first a blessing to the people around him, and it was by blessing others that he was promoted and eventually became prosperous himself. But even when Joseph became rich and powerful, he didn't use his wealth and power just to satisfy his every whim. He used his position to save his brothers and their families—the very people who sold him into slavery in the first place.

Joseph was a giver, and he always put God first—that's the same attitude we need to have. Today, when recession hits, the first thing most Christians cut back on is their giving, which is the absolute worst thing we can do. Like Joseph, we need to put God first regardless of our circumstances. In fact, when hard times come, we should increase our giving so that we can increase our harvest.

The Bible records that Isaac, Joseph's grandfather, sowed in a year of famine and reaped a hundredfold in return (Genesis 26:12). Almost everyone else had fled to Egypt from Canaan in search of food, but the Lord told Isaac to stay, and he obeyed. He decided to sow crops in the fields that had been abandoned by those who went looking for prosperity in the world, and he reaped a huge harvest. He became tremendously wealthy because he planted seed at a time when everyone else was holding back in fear of poverty.

These two stories are good illustrations of what we've been talking about: The reason God wants to bless us is so that we can be a blessing. If you come into a recession, cut back on your personal spending but never cut back on what you are doing for God. If God can get money through you, He will get it to you. Prosperity is having such an abundant supply that you are able to abound unto every good work, which means that blessings will flow your way when you are living to give.

> *Now he that ministereth seed to the sower both minister bread for your food, and multiply your seed sown, and increase the fruits of your righteousness.*

2 Corinthians 9:10

This verse isn't really about farming; it's an illustration of a spiritual principle. A single kernel of corn planted in the ground will sprout up a plant that bears thousands of kernels of corn. When you give money, it's like planting a seed. In the same way that planting a seed gives rise to a new plant that bears many more seeds, giving money away causes finances to grow in your life.

According to this scripture, God gives seed to the sower—just like God gave Isaac a hundredfold return on the crop he planted during a drought. The people who abandoned their fields and ran off to Egypt in search of prosperity didn't receive anything. God gave the return to Isaac because he sowed. When you give money, it's like planting a seed. God gives money to people if they are givers.

We also are told in God's Word, "For the eyes of the LORD run to and fro throughout the whole earth, to shew himself strong in the behalf of them whose heart is perfect toward him" (2 Chronicles 16:9). The word *perfect* here means "complete…whole…at peace."[12] It isn't talking about being sinless; it's talking about having a mature

---

[12] Brown, Driver, Briggs and Gesenius, *The KJV Old Testament Hebrew Lexicon,* "Hebrew Lexicon entry for Shalem," available from http://www. biblestudytools.com/lexicons/hebrew/kjv/shalem.html, S.V. "perfect," 2 Chronicles 16:9.

heart with a right attitude toward God. The Lord is searching the earth, looking for people who will believe His promises and put first the kingdom of God. He is looking for people who will give genuinely, from the heart, not as a form of manipulation—not giving just to get. God is literally searching the world for people He can give finances to; people who are givers.

You could turn this around and say that if you are consistently short on money, if you always have more month than you have money, then maybe God doesn't see you as a giver. That's not the only reason for experiencing lack. I've already shared how, at one time, I was struggling with lack because of wrong teaching I believed, so other things could be going on to cause lack in our lives, but it's also possible that our hearts aren't right.

There are two dominant heart conditions when it comes to money: eaters and sowers. *Eaters* are the ones who are all about getting their own needs met; they are seeking to establish their own kingdom. They use their resources to buy everything they want, and they only give when there is something leftover. *Sowers*, on the other hand, are all about putting other people first. Sowers need to eat too, so it's not like they can't buy things for themselves, but their hearts' desire is to give and seek God's kingdom first. *Sowers* are the people God is searching the world to find.

I saw a great example of this when I was ministering at a church a long time ago. The pastor told his people that he believed God had laid it on his heart for their church to give a $50,000 donation to us that week. At the time, we were believing for extra finances to finish out a new building and $50,000 would have been a huge gift. The pastor stood in front of his church and read 2 Corinthians 9:10 that says God, "ministereth seed to the sower." Then he asked, "How many of you would give $1,000 in this offering if God gave you the money?" About 50 people stood up to say that they would give if God gave them the money, and the pastor then prayed for finances to come to them.

Within a couple of days, some of those people started sharing testimonies of how God was supernaturally providing money. There wasn't a single person who only got $1,000 either. God was giving people two and three thousand dollars, so after they gave $1,000 in the offering, they still had plenty of money leftover. It was awesome! God doesn't just give you enough money to bless others. He always blesses you with extra.

The pastor collected the offering on a Monday night. One of the men who stood up and wanted to give $1,000 was going to give the money from his savings, but when he went into work on Monday morning, he got a promotion. I forget all the details, but his monthly income jumped by like $4,000 a month! He wanted to give a one-time offering of $1,000 and God multiplied his income for every month of the year.

As the testimonies came rolling in, other people began to realize that the givers weren't losing money by giving—they were actually making money. All of a sudden, other people started popping up and saying, "I want to pledge to give $1,000 too." From what I understood later, not many of those people who gave after they heard the testimonies saw God give them finances. I believe it's because their hearts were wrong. They weren't trying to put God's kingdom first by giving; they just wanted to make some extra money. It was selfish. Going to another scripture in Paul's letter to the Corinthians we see that giving profits you nothing if you don't do it motivated by love—even if you give all of your goods to feed the poor (1 Corinthians 13:3).

When we understand finances properly, we realize that prosperity isn't about us. It's about being able to bless other people. If you don't currently have that attitude, once you get it, you'll experience the reality that God gives seed to the sower. Selfishness short-circuits prosperity because it causes us to consume all of our resources. It turns us into a vacuum cleaner that sucks up everything in sight. We ought to be just the opposite.

> *If God can get money through you, He'll get it to you—and it won't be long before you have plenty leftover for yourself.*

Christians should be like leaf blowers: giving money left and right. We should be imitating God by searching for opportunities to give and asking Him to show us how we can be a blessing.

Another thing to keep in mind is that prosperity doesn't happen overnight. You don't go from being selfish to becoming a generous millionaire instantly for a couple of reasons. First, there is a time between planting seed and harvesting. Fruit doesn't show up the next day. Second, money has power, and you might not be able to handle the power of prosperity right away.

God knows you have needs, and He wants you to be taken care of. Remember, He doesn't mind if you live in a nice house and drive a nice car, as long as you aren't consuming all of your finances on yourself. When you get the attitude of a giver and walk it out over time, God will increase your finances. If God can get money through you, He'll get it to you—and it won't be long before you have plenty leftover for yourself.

Chapter 7

The Tithe

I was taught to believe that the tithe is mandatory.[13] We were told that we owed God a tenth of our income and if we didn't pay up, we'd be cursed. Not tithing, we were told, is the same as stealing from God. "You're robbing from God," they'd tell us, "and God is going to get you." Fortunately, none of that is true. God loves us independent of our performance, which includes whether or not we tithe. New Testament giving isn't a debt or an obligation.

> *This I say, He which soweth sparingly shall reap also sparingly; and he which soweth bountifully shall reap also bountifully. Every man according as he purposeth in his heart, so let him give; not grudgingly, or of necessity: for God loveth a cheerful giver.*
>
> *2 Corinthians 9:6–7*

I don't know how any Christian can read this passage and still think we are obligated to tithe or that we are cursed if we don't. It says we're not supposed to give "grudgingly, or of necessity." If the reason you pay a tithe is because you don't want to be under a

---

[13] Tithe means a tenth part, and tithing is the act of giving a tenth of your income back to God.

curse, then you are paying out of necessity and it isn't cheerful. It's like paying hush money to God.

We've all heard the stories about how the Mafia collects protection money from businesses. They come in and talk about how there has been a rash of break-ins or fires in the area, but they can make sure nothing happens to *your* business as long as you pay them cash every month. Of course, they're the ones committing all of the robberies and arson, but if you pay them, they won't destroy you too. In a sense, that's what preachers are teaching when they say you are cursed if you don't pay the tithe. They are saying you have to tithe to keep the curse off of your life. It's like paying the godfather, instead of God the Father. If that is why you are giving, then you are totally violating the motive given in this scripture.

We just saw that the Word tells us not to give grudgingly or of necessity because God loves a cheerful giver. The dominant motive for giving under the New Covenant should be a cheerful heart. We should be giving because we want to, not to pay God hush money.

The apostle Paul ends his teaching on giving in 2 Corinthians 9 by saying, "Thanks be unto God for his unspeakable gift" (v. 15). This summarizes why we should give back to the Lord under the New Covenant: because He has already given to us beyond measure. God has provided everything for us, and our giving is actually an expression of appreciation for all that He has done for us. It goes back to the scripture that says nothing we do is of any benefit unless it is motivated by love (1 Corinthians 13:3). Again, the motive behind our gift is more important than our gift.

Some ministers are vicious about the tithe. They harp on the curse of not tithing and talk about the wrath of God. I hate to disappoint those people, but Scripture says we have been "redeemed from the curse of the law" (Galatians 3:13). God isn't mad at you if you don't tithe—I think it's unwise not to tithe, but God will still love you if you don't.

Some people, reacting against the curse teaching, have swung in the completely opposite direction and say that the tithe was an Old Testament thing. They don't think it has any bearing on our lives today. I don't believe that is true. We're not cursed if we don't tithe, but tithing is still in our best interests.

The very first time the tithe was mentioned in Scripture was when Abraham gave tithes to Melchizedek, the king of Salem (Genesis 14:20). This was the same incident where Abraham refused to keep the king of Sodom's money because he didn't want anyone trying to say they made him rich (v. 23). Abraham knew that he was rich only because God had blessed him. This incident happened more than 400 years before Moses gave the Law to Israel.

You are not under a curse if you don't tithe.

We have been redeemed from the curse of the Law, and we aren't under the bondage of legalism to tithing, but we should also recognize that tithing was a biblical principle before the Law came along. Abraham wasn't living under the Law, yet he tithed. I believe that we are supposed to tithe too. Actually, I think the tithe is a starting place. Everything we have under the New Covenant is far superior to the Old Covenant, so I think we should be doing more than what was required under the Law.

Let's look at the classic passage from Malachi used to teach on the tithe.

Will a man rob God? Yet ye have robbed me. But ye say, Wherein have we robbed thee? In tithes and offerings. Ye are cursed with a curse: for ye have robbed me, even this whole nation. Bring ye all the tithes into the storehouse, that there may be meat in mine house, and prove me now herewith, saith the LORD of hosts, if I will not open you the windows of heaven, and pour you out a blessing, that there shall not be room enough to receive it. And I will rebuke the devourer for your sakes, and he shall not destroy the fruits of your ground; neither shall your vine cast her fruit before the time in the field, saith the LORD of hosts.

Malachi 3:8–11

Nearly everyone who teaches on the tithe cites this passage. Usually, it is used like a club to beat people into submission. But there is a huge difference between the punishment that came for disobeying the Law under the Old Covenant and the grace that we live under in the New Testament. The motivation for tithing today is out of appreciation for what God has done in our lives. It should come as a response of love from the heart, out of a desire to bless people. We don't tithe in an attempt to keep the Law. In fact, it would be a bad idea to even try.

For as many as are of the works of the law are under the curse: for it is written, Cursed is every one that continueth not in all things which are written in the book of the law to do them.

Galatians 3:10

You are cursed if you don't keep all of the Law. You can't just keep some of it, or do the best you can and God will make up the difference. No, if you don't keep every letter of the Law, then you are cursed! This is why Jesus came, because we are absolutely incapable of keeping the Law. It's impossible. The people who are trying to say you are cursed if you don't tithe are missing this point. You either trust the grace of God, or you reject Jesus' sacrifice and put your trust in your own performance and forfeit God's grace. You have to be 100 percent perfect—never making a single mistake in thought, word, or deed for your entire life—or you have to humble yourself and receive the gift of God's grace. Trying to satisfy the Law by paying a tithe isn't going to help.

> *But that no man is justified by the law in the sight of God,*
> *it is evident: for, The just shall live by faith. And the law is*
> *not of faith: but, The man that doeth them shall live in them.*
> *Christ hath redeemed us from the curse of the law, being*
> *made a curse for us: for it is written, Cursed is every one that*
> *hangeth on a tree: That the blessing of Abraham might come*
> *on the Gentiles through Jesus Christ; that we might receive*
> *the promise of the Spirit through faith.*

> *Galatians 3:11–14*

Yes, we have been redeemed from the curse of the Law! This passage couldn't be any clearer. It's true that the verse in Malachi 3 says you "are cursed with a curse" if you don't tithe, but this is exactly what we have been redeemed from. The whole attitude that God is going to punish you for not paying a tithe is completely unscriptural.

The church I went to as a child used to tell us that if we didn't pay our tithes, God would take it from us in doctors' bills. Either that or He would make our car break down, or our dishwasher stop working, or something else like that. I'm telling you, God doesn't relate to us that way under the New Covenant. Christ freed us from the curse of the Law. God is not coming against you. He is not going to take money from you if you don't tithe. Trying to pay off God like He's some kind of mobster is the wrong motivation. You're not going to benefit from that kind of giving.

It's also worth mentioning that the passage in Malachi 3:8–11 says the curse comes for robbing God in tithes *and* offerings. The ministers who use this verse to teach about tithing from a Law perspective conveniently overlook that you also have to give offerings to keep the Law. I've never personally sat down and figured it out, but I've heard other ministers say that the offerings added up to way more than the tithe. There were so many offerings that, all together, the mandatory giving totaled more like 33 percent. So if you are trying to live by the Law, you are cursed unless you are giving at least that percentage.

I've had a number of people criticize me over teaching that we aren't under the curse when we don't tithe, but they don't have anything to say when I point out that Malachi 3 mentions tithes *and* offerings. I can guarantee you that most of the people who are so adamant about the curse of the tithe are not giving 33 percent. But it's hypocritical to say you are cursed for not paying tithes and just leave the offerings out. Christ has redeemed us from the curse of the Law, so we're not cursed under the New Covenant for not tithing.

The motive for our giving has to be a cheerful heart, but we can see the natural reasons why tithing is beneficial. It's just like a farmer who sows seeds to reap a crop. God gives you seed, and you have a choice about what to do with that seed. You can eat all of the seed that God gives you, or you can plant some of it and reap a crop that will ensure you have something to eat next year. Planting seeds ensures a future crop, and tithing moves finances into your future—in addition to the eternal benefit. Money is like seed, and when you consume every dollar that comes your way, you aren't investing in your future.

God loves you if you eat all of your seed, but don't be surprised when the money runs out and you're crying out to God about not meeting your needs. It's not His fault if you ate all of your seed. You need to be disciplined enough to take a portion of what God has given you and sow it into your future. The tithe is a starting place; ultimately, you should desire to give even more than 10 percent. Remember, God is still going to love you whether you give nine percent, eleven percent, or nothing at all. Tithing has nothing to do with how God relates to you, but there is still a benefit to tithing.

We don't tithe to please God; we do it out of a sense of appreciation for all that God has done for us.

God the Father put all of His wrath on Jesus, so He isn't mad at you for not tithing. He's not even in a bad mood. Jesus became a curse so that we wouldn't be cursed. We aren't living under the bondage of the Law anymore. We don't tithe to please God; we do it out of a sense of appreciation for all that God has done for us, and because it's the smart thing to do. I can't emphasize enough that there is no longer a punishment associated with tithing, and it doesn't change how God sees us.

But just because the punishment for not tithing has been taken away, doesn't mean we should stop giving. It's similar to how parents teach children to do the right thing by using punishment, or the threat of it, to keep their kids in line. I grew up on a busy road and my mother used to threaten to spank me if I ever crossed the street without looking both ways. Actually, she had to do that to me a number of times! She did it because she loved me, and she didn't want me getting hit by a car. My mother isn't around to spank me anymore, but I still look both ways before crossing the street because it's the smart thing to do.

This is a lot like the difference between how God related to Israel under the Old Covenant and how He deals with Christians under the New Covenant. Old Testament believers didn't have the spiritual capacity to understand why they should or shouldn't do certain things because the natural mind can't understand the things of God.

> *The natural man receiveth not the things of the Spirit of God: for they are foolishness unto him: neither can he know them, because they are spiritually discerned.*

> *1 Corinthians 2:14*

The people under the Law were spiritually dead, as all people are until they are born again by believing in Jesus. God couldn't explain to them the spiritual benefits of godly behavior so, in a sense, God treated them like children and threatened punishment to keep them from hurting themselves. You can't reason with a toddler, but you also can't wait until a child is twenty years old before you start teaching him or her the difference between right and wrong. So you use punishment as a tool until he or she is old enough to understand reason. But punishment is only a temporary fix. You won't, or shouldn't, still be doing the right thing out of fear of punishment when you are fifty or sixty years old. Something would be seriously wrong if you were. As an adult, you do the right thing because you understand that actions have consequences.

This is the way it was with mankind. Prior to Jesus coming and bringing the new birth, people didn't have the right heart motives and they couldn't understand spiritual things, so God just told them what to do and enforced it with punishment. That's why the book of Malachi said that the people of Israel would be under a curse if they didn't tithe. Even a lost man could understand that it was in his best interests to tithe when the alternative was to be cursed.

Now that we are born again and God's Spirit lives in us, He has removed the curse. It's like we're adults now, and He is no longer trying to get us to behave by threatening punishment. Now, we do what is right out of a good heart and because we understand spiritual things. I give tithes and offerings because it's a way of showing my faith and using the finances God gave me to help build His kingdom. I believe in tithing just like I still look both ways before crossing the street; I just give with a different motivation than they did under the Old Covenant.

A long time ago, a man heard me preach on how giving out of a sense of obligation profits you nothing, and he decided to change how he was giving. He was the kind who wrote out his tithe check down to the penny. The bottom line was that he was tithing because he felt obligated to give God ten percent of his income. At the time, he was making around $3,000 a month, which was a lot of money back then, but he still felt like he was always behind financially. So after hearing me teach, he and his wife decided they were going to start giving as they purposed in their heart. He stopped calculating his tithe exactly, and they just started giving whatever they wanted.

About six months later, he realized that they had more money in the bank than they'd ever had before. His first thought was, *I bet I've decreased my giving.* Prior to his change of heart, he paid his tithe like a bill. He put it in the same column as all of his other debts and paid it every month like clockwork. By his thinking, extra money in his account meant he must not have been paying his "tithing bill." So he went back and added together his checks over the past six months to see how much he had been giving. What he discovered surprised him: he had moved his giving up to 24 percent of his income. He was giving more than twice as much as he ever had, yet he was more prosperous than ever—because God was prospering him supernaturally.

When you give grudgingly or out of necessity or because you think God is going to break your kneecaps if you don't pay up, it profits you nothing. You get zero benefit from that kind of giving. The people you give to will benefit, but it isn't going to come back to you. That kind of giving won't influence your future. You have to come out from under the mindset of Old Testament obligation and start giving with a joyful heart if you want to see a return on your giving.

Jesus said, "Give, and it shall be given unto you; good measure, pressed down, and shaken together, and running over, shall men give into your bosom. For with the same measure that ye mete withal it shall be measured to you again" (Luke 6:38). But if that was all there was to prosperity, then nearly every Christian would be prosperous. If all you had to do was give and, *boom*, it came back to you a hundredfold, then every church would be packed full with millionaires. You'd probably be surprised at the total if

God loves a cheerful giver!

you were to take all that you have given in your lifetime and multiply it by 100; every ten grand you have given equals a million dollars in return. So why hasn't every believer seen that kind of return? The reason is that the motive behind your gift is more important than the gift itself.

Some people have been giving faithfully for a long time, but they've been doing it with the wrong motivation. They've been taught they should tithe out of obligation and they've just been paying a bill, or they've been doing it to appease God. That kind of giving benefits the church you are writing your checks to, but it isn't going to benefit you in this life. You won't get a hundredfold return on that giving. You have to plant your financial seed with a cheerful heart, motivated by love, because your gift is ruined when you give with the wrong motive.

I believe that tithing is a godly thing and that all Christians should tithe. In the Old Testament, they gave because they had to, but our giving should flow from a revelation of God's love for us. I don't want anyone to think I'm saying that Christians are free from the tithe or that we shouldn't be giving back to the Lord. I'm just saying that we need to purify our motives. Actually, I think that if Old Testament believers gave 10 percent, then New Testament saints should be giving at least that much. But we need to learn to give cheerfully.

Since the wrong motivation voids our giving, it's better to give God one percent or two percent cheerfully, than to give ten percent with the wrong attitude. Let's say you have a hundred seeds. Would it be better to plant ten of those seeds and have nothing grow, or to plant one seed that actually produces a crop? It would be better to plant one seed that produces fruit than to plant ten seeds that don't produce anything. The same is true with your giving: it would be better to give a little with the right motivation than to give 10 percent without any benefit. It would also build your faith to see a return come from giving with the right motive. We saw earlier that the Lord talked about this saying,

> *Bring ye all the tithes into the storehouse, that there may be meat in mine house, and prove me now herewith, saith the LORD of hosts, if I will not open you the windows of heaven, and pour you out a blessing, that there shall not be room enough to receive it.*

> *Malachi 3:10*

As far as I know, this is the only instance in Scripture where the Lord says, "Prove Me." Basically, He's saying, *"Try it, and see if it doesn't work!"* Nearly everything else He said was a command: Thou shalt do this, or thou shalt not do that. But when it comes to tithing, He said, "Prove Me." I think that He said it this way because He knows it is scary for people to take a portion of what they need to survive and give it away. When you are dependent upon money to pay bills and buy food, it's hard to move your trust over to a God you can't see. God knows that about us, so He said, "Try Me."

When you first start giving, it might be better for you to give two or five percent if that is what you can trust God with and do it with joy and peace. If that is what you can give cheerfully, then start there. It's better to give a small percentage cheerfully than to tithe in fear. Ultimately, I think we should be giving more than ten percent, but you should start where you are comfortable—or where you purpose in your heart (2 Corinthians 9:7).

I'm not encouraging people who are giving ten percent to drop down in their giving. I'm just saying that the motive behind your gift is more important than the quantity of the gift. So if you need to drop back until your faith can build up and you can give ten percent with a good heart, then do it. But eventually, you want to get to where you are thinking, *God, this is Your money. What do You want me to do with it?* It all comes down to the motive of your heart.

Giving out of fear is the same thing as giving "grudgingly," and giving out of manipulation and condemnation is the same as giving "of necessity" (v. 7). Giving with those motives profits you nothing. Unfortunately, you sometimes hear ministers at church or on television manipulating people into giving "of necessity." I actually heard someone on a television fundraiser say that if anyone gave $1,000 within the next ten minutes then God was going to open up the heavens and pour out all kinds of blessings. That's not fundraising, it's bribery! Besides, Jesus already opened the heavens for us, and nothing we do changes that. Sure enough, when the ten minutes were up, the television minister said, "I believe the Lord is extending the window another seven minutes." I'm telling you, it would be funny if it wasn't so pathetic how some believers are manipulated into giving.

The sad part is that these ministers only do that kind of stuff because it works. On the whole, the body of Christ is so immature in financial matters that people will fall for anything. Then the ministers look at the response they get and say, "It worked! Do it again!" Now we have people making hundreds of millions of dollars because believers are giving toward manipulation and thinking they can buy the blessings of God. "You've got to get in on this giving in the next five minutes," they say, "because after that, God is going to cut off His blessings." But the blessings of God don't come with an expiration date.

Christians shouldn't fall for that kind of coercion. The only giving that is acceptable to God is that which you purpose in your own heart and give cheerfully—not grudgingly or of necessity. You aren't going to buy prosperity from God or force Him into blessing you—just like you don't need to pay Him protection money to keep the curse of the Law out of your life. All of that is manipulation and condemnation, and giving with those motivations profits you nothing.

When I was eighteen years old, I went to hear a man speak at a denominational church in Texas. He said, "If you were going to a movie, you'd pay $3 to get in. I don't want some people giving $20 or $50 in this offering; I just want every person in here to give $3."

(Paying $3 for a movie ticket tells you how long ago this was!) He said, "I want everybody to get their $3 and hold it up in their hand so I can see. If you don't have it, then borrow it from your neighbor. We're going to wait until everybody has their $3 up."

I had just gotten really fired up about the Lord at that time in my life, and I was sitting on the front row. I had $3 in my wallet too, but I wasn't about to give in response to an offering like that. So I sat in the front row with my arms folded across my chest, looking the pastor in the eye and thinking, *I dare you to point me out and make an issue of it. Give me an opportunity, and I'll stand up in front of this crowd and rebuke you!* He never did look at me, but he continued to pressure people to hold up their $3.

Some people might think I had a bad attitude, but I didn't. I defied him because I feel that kind of manipulation is wrong, and every time you give in it's like voting for a politician. That person gets into power and continues to do what got him there. Well, if you voted for that individual, then you've got no right to complain about how he operates. You're the one who empowered him. Likewise, if the body of Christ would quit giving to people who use manipulation, then those ministers would be out of business; they wouldn't be on television or in the pulpit, and they wouldn't be in a position to continue manipulating people.

Several of the organizations that use those tactics receive a lot of money every year. They have learned how to influence people into giving them money. It's wrong, but it isn't going to change unless we learn to give with the right motivation. Remember, Scripture says that we should be motivated by love in our giving, not guilt. *God loves a cheerful giver!*

I encourage you to give and to tithe, but don't do it out of fear or guilt, do it because you love God and you want to show your appreciation for all that He has done for you. When you purify your motives for tithing and start doing it as you desire in your heart, I believe that then you'll begin to see the hundredfold return on your giving—and you'll probably find yourself wanting to give a lot more than ten percent.

Chapter 8

Give Where You're Fed

A lot of people are confused about where they should give their tithes and offerings or how the money they give should be used. We've seen that Scripture says, "Bring ye all the tithes into the storehouse" (Malachi 3:10). In the Old Testament, the tithe was given toward the work of God. It was either given to a priest who offered the sacrifices, or it was brought directly to the Temple (for those who lived in Jerusalem). There were other offerings the people had to pay for, but the tithe went directly to the ministers; that was how God supported the ministers who were doing His work.

Most pastors teach that the storehouse is your local church and that parachurch and other social-welfare ministries are meant to be supported by offerings that are over and above the tithe. In a perfect world, I'd have to agree with that, but we don't live in a perfect world. Technically, a storehouse is where you put your food. In Old Testament times, it was where they would hang meat and store grain, and when they got hungry they would go there to get something to eat. You could say that a storehouse is where you get fed—so you should be giving your tithe where you get fed, spiritually speaking, and that may not be your local church.

However, we have to recognize that churches do more than just teach the Word. A church fosters community and is an important part of spiritual growth. We need the maturity that comes through fellowshipping with other believers. A good local church helps us raise our children and gives them a place to meet other Christian kids. It offers one-on-one counseling and marriage counseling. Our local pastors help us deal with grief and get through hard times.

A good local church does many things that a television minister can't do for you. For instance, I am on television, but you can't call me in the middle of the night when tragedy strikes. You can't meet at my house and fellowship with other believers, and I can't bring you food when a loved one dies. So if you are in a good local church that is preaching the Word, helping widows and orphans, and doing what a godly church is supposed to do, then you should be tithing at your church—no question about it.

Unfortunately, I don't believe a large number of churches are teaching about the grace of God and preaching the true Gospel. The most common question I get is from people who are looking for a church that is teaching about the love of God and the finished work of Jesus. From what I can tell, I would say that the majority of believers are not in a church that is truly preaching the Word of God. Many people are going to churches they know aren't good, but they go there out of a sense of obligation or because there are no other options. Maybe their whole family goes to that particular church, or it's the one they've always gone to and they don't want to change.

In fact, a lot of people are going to churches that preach things completely contrary to the Gospel message. They leave church feeling condemned and beat up—the exact opposite of what a church is supposed to do. It would be wrong for me to tell you to put your tithes into the local church and not qualify that by saying a *good* local church, one that is meeting the needs of its members.

It matters where you plant your seed. Some people think that God sees their heart when they give, and they reap a benefit from their giving regardless of what the church does with their money, but that's not true. You'd be a very poor farmer with that kind of attitude. You can't expect the same results from casting your seed on pavement that you would get from planting it in fertile soil. In addition, every time you give to a church or minister, you are casting a vote in support of how they conduct themselves. Every time you give money to a church, you are helping support what they do—whether it's good or bad—so it absolutely matters where you give your money.

I'm not saying the church has to be perfect—no church is. Maybe your church isn't hitting on all cylinders, but they are preaching the truth and being a light to the community. In that case, I would recommend giving your tithe there because you need what a local church offers. But if you feel worse after you go to church than you did when you went in or if the church is supporting causes that are contrary to the Word or not doing anything in the community, then you shouldn't be subsidizing that with your giving.

Scripture tells us to bring our tithes into the storehouse, so we should be giving where we get fed. It's wrong to put your money into something that you don't agree with, and then go get fed by ministries you don't support. That's like eating at a restaurant and going across the street to a different one to pay for your meal. No, you pay your bill where you ate—and you should give your tithe where you get spiritually fed. If you aren't being fed at your church, then you shouldn't be tithing there.

I travel a lot. It's not uncommon for me to be out of town three Sundays every month. So I'm not at my local church every weekend. I give to the local church when I'm there, but I don't give an exact tithe of my income because I may only be there six or seven times in an entire year. I don't get fed by my church much (because of my absence), and my kids are grown, so we spread our giving around. I give God well more than ten percent of my income, but I split my tithing and giving among my church and the other ministries that feed me.

Where you give your money is important.

We also need to keep in mind that giving where we are fed can't be the only criteria for our giving. If that was the only reason for giving, then missionaries who work in faraway countries wouldn't have any income and no one would be helping widows and orphans. The people missionaries help are often impoverished and unable to support them. Missionaries need financial partners who will help them spread the Gospel, but who don't directly benefit from their ministry. So giving where you are fed isn't the only guideline for tithing, but I believe it should be the primary one.

Your tithe, or at least a portion of it, should be going to the ministry that is feeding you. However, widows and orphans may not minister to you, but it is a godly thing to give and support them—that falls under what is called *benevolence giving* (1 Timothy 5:3–10; James 1:27). There is also giving that goes toward missionary work. So not all of your giving should go to where you are being fed, but the bulk of it should.

A good local church will feed you in ways that no other ministry can. The body of Christ is dependent upon the local church. If we didn't have local churches to meet our needs and we were solely dependent upon television preachers (of which I'm one), then the body of Christ would be in a crisis situation. The local church is the backbone of the body, and it's best for you to be in a good local church where you can give your tithe—but don't put your tithe into a dead church.

In the first place, if you are in a dead church, get out! Go find yourself a church that is preaching the Gospel and then put your tithe into that church and use offerings to support other parts of the body of Christ. Maybe you live in a rural area with limited options, or your spouse will only go to one certain church, or something else keeps you tied to a church that isn't preaching the Gospel. If for some reason you can't find a good local church or get out of the dead one you're in, then, at a minimum, you shouldn't give all of your money there. The best option is to get out of the dead church, but if you can't—or won't—do that, then you should at least split your tithe.

This principle of giving where you are fed is really simple, and it would solve a lot of problems if believers followed it. The preachers who are lying and manipulating people in order to get money are not truly feeding the body of Christ. They would go out of business if we'd just stop giving them money. They'd have to come up with some other con and move on with their lives. Then the people who are really feeding Christians would be getting all of the resources and we would have an abundance of finances. The good churches wouldn't have to hold car washes and bake sales to raise money.

Our television show has the potential of reaching three billion people on a daily basis. I don't know what percentage of that potential actually watches, but let's just say it's one percent, which is thirty million people. If thirty million people were being encouraged and built up in the Word by our ministry and they started sending us money because we are feeding them, I'm not sure we'd know what to do with it all. Yet only a very small percentage of our viewers give to the ministry. I'm sure there are lots of people who are getting fed by us, but they are giving their money elsewhere because they don't know this simple principle of giving where you are fed.

Your return is going to depend to a degree on how fruitful the ground is that you are sowing into.

Giving where you are fed makes a difference for you too. The return on your giving is going to depend to a degree on how fruitful the ground is that you are sowing into, just like there is a difference between planting in concrete and dirt. If you give to a church or ministry that isn't really accomplishing the Lord's work (concrete), then you are going to get marginal returns. When you plant your seed in a place that is fruitful and ministering the Word of God (dirt), then you are going to receive a better return. Don't give where you are begged or pressured, or where you've always given—give where you are fed. Bring the tithes into the storehouse! Wherever you get your food from is where you should be giving; it's that simple.

Quit giving where you are coerced, intimidated, and condemned. I actually had a woman come to me one time with a personalized letter that said, "*Dear Stella*—or whatever her name was—*God woke me up at three o'clock this morning and gave me your name and told me to tell you that if you send me $1,000, then all of the people you have been praying for will get saved.*" The letter went on to promise healing, prosperity, and deliverance if she would just send in some money.

She was a poor woman and she told me that she could scrape together the $1,000, but she wasn't really sure she should give it. On the other hand, she felt compelled to because the letter was personalized and the minister claimed God woke him up at three in the morning with a special message for her. She said, "What should I do?" I just took the letter and tore it up. I had to explain that the exact same computer-generated letter was probably sent to thousands of people. The reason ministers who are unscrupulous send those kinds of letters is that Christians actually give them money in response.

I hate to say it, but I believe the majority of giving in the body of Christ is in response to begging or some sort of emotional coercion. Some preachers are raising a lot of money by manipulating people and doing all kinds of ungodly things, and it bothers me that Christians respond to that. The body of Christ is empowering those preachers and perpetuating all of that manipulation by giving money to support it. It's possible for some good to come out of that kind of giving because God can use anything, but those practices are wrong. If we would learn the biblical guidelines for when and why to give, then we would starve out the charlatans. The people who are truly preaching the Word of God would have such an abundance that they would never have to mention money again.

Giving out of desperation because somebody said that God would supply your needs is an ungodly principle. In a sense, it's like trying to buy a miracle. As a matter of fact, the book of Acts tells a story about a man named Simon who tried to do the same thing. Simon had been a magician in Samaria, but he was born again when he heard Philip preach the Gospel. Later, Peter and John went down to Samaria and prayed for people to receive the Holy Spirit. Simon saw that people were receiving the gift of speaking in tongues when Peter and John laid hands on them. Simon also wanted to be able lay hands on people and have them receive the Holy Spirit, so he offered Peter money to give him the same gift. On the surface, that seems like a good desire, but Peter responded differently. He said,

> *Thy money perish with thee, because thou hast thought that the gift of God may be purchased with money. Thou hast neither part nor lot in this matter: for thy heart is not right in the sight of God....For I perceive that thou art in the gall of bitterness, and in the bond of iniquity.*

> *Acts 8:20–21, 23*

I'm not sure whether being in the "gall of bitterness, and in the bond of iniquity" means that Simon was never really born again, or whether his heart was just wrong, but it's not good either way.

Simon thought he could buy God's anointing by giving Peter money, and Peter rebuked him. This shows that our heart is not right if we are trying to buy God's blessings. At the same time, it's possible to be in the process of believing God for a miracle, and it may be that letting go of some of your money could be a step of faith for you. See, it isn't giving money that makes the miracle happen—it's stepping out in faith.

A lot of people only give when they're begged—partly because that's what they've been taught. When Jamie and I first moved to Colorado Springs, a man gave our ministry a building and then came to work for us for about six months. Back then, we used to send out teachings on tape cassettes. He noticed that we would fill as many orders for tapes as we could for a couple of weeks at a time, but then we'd run out of money and we'd have to wait a week or two until we had enough money to get in another shipment of blank tapes. Then we would duplicate more teachings and start filling orders again.

When he saw what was going on, he asked me why I wasn't telling people how desperate the ministry was for additional finances. He told me he had given away $25,000 the previous year, and he always asked God where to send the money before he gave. He said I was the first person who came to mind every time he prayed because our ministry had helped him transform his life, but he didn't give to us because I never asked. Do you know who he gave to? He gave to a television minister who was always begging for money and telling people he was going to go off the air if they didn't give.

I was invited to be a guest on that same minister's network much later and the head of his ministry showed me a room filled with thousands of letters stuffed and sealed in envelopes. All they had to do was slap a stamp and an address on the envelopes and mail them out. The letters talked about a pending financial crisis if people didn't give. They sent out those letters on six-month intervals and they had printed out "crisis letters" two years in advance. *They didn't even have a crisis yet!* It was all lies and manipulation. They begged, and people gave.

We're not supposed to give where we are begged—we're supposed to give as we purpose in our own heart. Not just that, but we're supposed to give where we are fed. The people who are using manipulation are not truly in tune with God. I'm not saying they aren't born again, but I'm saying they are carnal. Those people aren't really feeding the body of Christ. If we'd stop giving to them, they would go away.

I had a publicity group come to me one time and guarantee that they could raise $1 million by sending out letters for us. It was back when our income was about $80,000 a month, and we needed the extra income so I told them I would fly them out and meet with them. They started by telling me about the color ink that people respond to, the font we should use, and how to underline certain statements; they had the whole business down to a science. They also told me how they had raised another client $20 million just a couple of months before using the same techniques.

I said, "Well, we could sure use $20 million. But what are you going to say? What are you going to do?"

They said, "Just leave that up to us."

"No," I said, "I need to know what you are going to say."

So they started telling me how they would put in a picture of children with distended bellies and flies crawling all over them. Then they'd say we help support orphanages and things like that.

I said, "But I don't support any orphanages."

"Neither does the guy we raised the $20 million for," they said.

I told them I wasn't interested in using dishonest practices. They argued that once I had the money I could use it any way I wanted to, but I wasn't going to compromise. My integrity is more important to me than getting millions of dollars, so I sent them away. But the reason those people are in business is because what they do works.

It's okay to give when you are touched emotionally sometimes, but don't let that be the driving motivation behind your giving. If you aren't already doing so, you should give from your firstfruits and give where you are fed. Give to the people who have really affected your life. If the body of Christ would start doing that, then the people who are truly ministering the Word of God would have a superabundance and the charlatans would have to repent or get out of ministry. It would also increase the harvest you receive on your giving—because just like a farmer reaps a bigger harvest by planting in fertile soil, your giving achieves better returns when you plant it in a ministry that is doing kingdom work.

Chapter 9

Partnership

One of the best-known scriptures about prosperity is the apostle Paul's statement to the Philippians that "my God shall supply all your need" (Philippians 4:19). Often, you hear that verse taught like it applies to every person on the face of the planet. It's true that God wants to supply all of your needs, and there are plenty of scriptures that talk about that—like how God provides for the birds of the air and the lilies of the field (Matthew 6:25–30)—but Paul wrote this particular verse about people who had partnered with him in spreading the Gospel. He was talking about the special blessing on partnership. Earlier in his letter, Paul said,

> *I thank my God upon every remembrance of you, always in every prayer of mine for you all making request with joy, for your fellowship in the gospel from the first day until now.*

> *Philippians 1:3–5*

The word translated *fellowship* in verse 5 is the Greek word *koinonia*, and it means "partnership."[14] Paul was thanking the

---

[14] Based on information from Thayer and Smith, "Greek Lexicon entry for Koinonia," available http://www.biblestudytools.com/lexicons/greek/kjv/koinonia.html, S.V. "partnership," Philippians 1:5.

Philippians for their partnership in the Gospel. They were people who gave to Paul in a greater way than any other church had. Paul made specific mention of how eager they were to care for him and provide for his needs.

I rejoiced in the LORD greatly, that now at the last your care of me hath flourished again; wherein ye were also careful, but ye lacked opportunity.

Philippians 4:10

The Philippians were regular supporters of Paul as he traveled from place to place preaching the Good News. They were helping him carry the Gospel to other areas around the world. When he said they were careful but lacked opportunity, he was saying that they didn't always know where to send their money. Paul had been arrested in Jerusalem, locked in prison, and shipwrecked on his way to trial in Rome. Basically, his location was constantly changing for about three years. They didn't have the communications to know exactly where Paul was, so they "lacked opportunity" to give. But the moment they heard Paul was in Rome, they sent clothes, finances, and things for him to study. They were eager to help him, but Paul wasn't rejoicing over them just because they took care of him.

Not that I speak in respect of want: for I have learned, in whatsoever state I am, therewith to be content. I know both how to be abased, and I know how to abound: every where and in all things I am instructed both to be full and to be hungry, both to abound and to suffer need. I can do all things through Christ which strengtheneth me.

Philippians 4:11–13

Paul said that he had learned how to live in need and abundance. He was rejoicing because he saw their heart to give, and he knew that by supporting him they were actually giving to God. He saw that their giving would cause God to pour out a blessing on them and result in a hundredfold return. He went on to say:

> *Notwithstanding ye have well done, that ye did communicate*
> *with my affliction. Now ye Philippians know also, that*
> *in the beginning of the gospel, when I departed from*
> *Macedonia, no church communicated with me as concerning*
> *giving and receiving, but ye only.*

> *Philippians 4:14–15*

When he says *communicated*, Paul is talking about how they gave financially. The amazing thing here is that Paul says no other churches were giving him money to help preach the Gospel—only the Philippians! Paul and his companions were in constant jeopardy, and they endured great persecution and suffering to preach the Good News, but none of the other churches Paul started were supporting him in his work. I think that's tragic.

It seems people gave to Paul only while he was in their town preaching. They fed him and gave him a place to stay, but as soon as he left town he was on his own again. So every time he went to a new place he had to start all over financially. I don't think Paul should have been scraping by like that. People should have been so thankful for what God was doing through him that they took care of Paul no matter where he was, but only the Philippians blessed Paul after he went away. You can see why Paul was thankful every time he thought about the Philippians and how they helped establish churches in other areas.

For even in Thessalonica ye sent once and again unto my necessity. Not because I desire a gift: but I desire fruit that may abound to your account.

Philippians 4:16–17

"Once and again" just means they sent money to Paul more than once. It's a good thing too, because Paul's ministry wasn't well received in Thessalonica. He was basically run out of town (Acts 17). So if it wasn't for the financial support of the Philippians, he might not have been able to continue his ministry there. Their giving wasn't just benefiting Paul personally; it was helping to establish God's kingdom abroad, and Paul was rejoicing because he knew that God gives prosperity to help establish His covenant. Paul understood that their giving would result in a supernatural return—because God gives seed to sowers (2 Corinthians 9:10).

Paul talked about how their giving caused him to abound, and then he said,

But my God shall supply all your need according to his riches in glory by Christ Jesus.

Philippians 4:19

There is no doubt that God delights in the prosperity of His servants, or that He sends sun and rain on the just and the unjust alike (Psalm 35:27; Matthew 5:45; 3 John 2). God desires to bless both believers and unbelievers, but this particular verse in

Philippians 4 is talking about people who had partnered with Paul in sharing the Gospel and were helping to establish God's covenant upon the earth. They weren't just giving to Paul because they were receiving from him. They were giving when Paul was blessing people beyond their own city, and they weren't receiving anything in return. In modern terms, you could say that they weren't just giving to get books, CDs, and DVDs—they were giving toward missionary work.

Philippians 4:19 is talking about the special blessing on those who become partners in spreading the Gospel, which means that if you really want to be blessed, then partner with a ministry that has a big vision and is doing a great job of spreading the Gospel. The way God gets money to a ministry is by giving it to the believers who support it. In order for the money to get to the ministry, it has to pass through the hands of partners first—"and as the money passes through, there will be plenty leftover for you." So one of the best ways to prosper is to find a ministry that is powerfully anointed by God and become a partner with it.

I couldn't provide one week's worth of the income it takes to run our ministry. It takes the support of our partners to supply our financial needs and enable us to do what God has called us to do. I know that our partners have to prosper before our ministry can prosper, so I pray that God blesses our partners and causes them to abound. The reason is that ability to accomplish God's will is directly dependent upon other people joining with me and becoming partners. All of the money God needs to get to our ministry has to come through our partners first. The same is true for every other ministry out there.

This is why God can cause a supernatural flow of finances to go your way when you identify yourself as a giver. God has made provision for every believer, but there is a special anointing on people who give in order to help spread the Gospel. When you say, "I want to help this church change our city," or "I want to help this person go around the world and spread the Gospel," then God can prosper you to do that. God gives money to people who will use it to advance the kingdom (Deuteronomy 8:18), and He gives more than enough so there is always plenty leftover for the giver.

Aside from causing a flow of finances to pass through partners' hands, there is an additional benefit to partnering with a ministry.

A man's gift maketh room for him, and bringeth him before great men.

Proverbs 18:16

I used to think this scripture meant "gift" in the sense of God-given ability or anointing. I thought that if I would use my gift of teaching properly, for instance, it would open up doors and bring me before important, influential men and women. But the Hebrew word used for gift here is *mattan*, and it literally means "present." [15] It's clear from the other uses of his word in Scripture that it means some kind of monetary gift. (See Proverbs 15:27; 19:6.) It's not talking about the anointing on your life. This verse is simply saying that even in the natural realm, a gift opens up doors.

---

[15] Brown, Driver, Briggs and Gesenius, *The KJV Old Testament Hebrew Lexicon*, "Hebrew Lexicon entry for Mattan," available from http://www.biblestudytools.com/lexicons/hebrew/kjv/mattan.html, S.V. "gift," Proverbs 18:16.

In a negative sense, you could understand this kind of gift to be a bribe, but there is also a positive side to this; a gift doesn't have to be used in a negative way. You can turn away wrath with a gift or gain favor with others. Gifts also have an effect in the spiritual realm. When you give, it opens up doors for you. It can create opportunities and bring you before powerful people. This is different from a bribe, and Scripture gives us an example of a gift being used in this positive sense.

In the Old Testament, it says that when the Queen of Sheba heard how wise and prosperous King Solomon was, she traveled to Jerusalem to witness it for herself. It tells us that she went up "with a very great train" of camels bearing spices, precious stones, and "very much gold" (1 Kings 10:2). The Queen of Sheba was astounded by what she saw in King Solomon's court, and she said to him,

> *It was a true report that I heard in mine own land of thy acts and of thy wisdom. Howbeit I believed not the words, until I came, and mine eyes had seen it: and, behold, the half was not told me: thy wisdom and prosperity exceedeth the fame which I heard.*

> *1 Kings 10:6–7*

Solomon was the wisest and wealthiest man on the face of the earth. The Bible says that people came from all over the world to inquire of him and search out his wisdom (v. 24). Think about that. Today, if you tried to meet with the president of the United States or the prime minister of Israel, do you think you would be able to walk right into his office and sit down? No way, there are protocols, and you have to get in line. I believe Solomon had more fame and notoriety than you could imagine the leader of any country having nowadays. So the Queen of Sheba brought gifts to gain Solomon's attention and gain access to him.

> *She gave the king an hundred and twenty talents of gold,*
> *and of spices very great store, and precious stones: there came*
> *no more such abundance of spices as these which the queen of*
> *Sheba gave to king Solomon.*

> *1 Kings 10:10*

A talent is equal to about 75.5 pounds, so that means she gave Solomon 9,000 pounds, or 145,000 ounces, of gold. At today's price of $1,730 per ounce (at the time of this writing), Solomon's gold would be worth more than $250 million, and there's no telling how much her other gifts were worth. I can guarantee a gift that size is going to make room for you. I don't know how long the line of people waiting to see King Solomon was, but the queen's gift moved her right to the front. Not only did she get to spend a little time with him, she ate with him and saw all the different aspects of his kingdom. The implication is that she was able to spend a number of days with Solomon. We don't know the exact details, but the queen's gift opened up a door. It made room for her and brought her before the greatest man of her day—that's the positive power of a gift.

In a spiritual sense, when you give by partnering with a ministry, it makes room for you. It's like you start drawing on the anointing that is on the ministry. You end up partaking of the fruits of the ministry. When you partner with someone who is preaching the Good News, then you receive the benefit of prospering from their blessing.

Here's something else to consider: most likely the Queen of Sheba could have used that $250 million for needs within her own kingdom. Can you imagine the length of the camel train she would have needed to carry all of those goods, plus the soldiers to guard it? They must have traveled to Jerusalem with hundreds of camels and an entourage the size of a small army. It couldn't have been inconspicuous, and the people in her kingdom probably wondered where she was going with all of that wealth. It must have raised some eyebrows when people heard that she was planning to give all of that money to a king who was already the richest man on earth.

I'm sure some people were thinking, *Why give so much money to King Solomon? Think of how many poor people she could help with that money.* She could have changed entire nations with that money. She could have built buildings and helped farmers in every town she passed through. But the Queen of Sheba decided she was going to use that money to go find out how King Solomon had become so successful in running his kingdom, then she could apply that knowledge to improving her own land. She passed up all of the beggars and cities that could have used her resources and brought them to the wealthiest man alive. She did it because she wanted to partake of the success Solomon was experiencing, and it worked.

> *King Solomon gave unto the queen of Sheba all her desire, whatsoever she asked, beside that which Solomon gave her of his royal bounty. So she turned and went to her own country, she and her servants.*
>
> *1 Kings 10:13*

It would be interesting to know how much of his royal bounty Solomon gave to the Queen of Sheba. The next verse tells us that Solomon received 666 talents of gold annually, plus the profits he made from businesses and the kings of other countries that paid him taxes—which means the Queen's gift was only a fraction of King Solomon's yearly earnings. Solomon was so rich he didn't even keep track of silver; they threw it on the streets and treated it like a rock. He was unbelievably wealthy. So when it says that Solomon gave to her of his bounty, I think the Queen of Sheba received more from Solomon than she gave. I think she left Jerusalem with more money than she had when she came.

As the Queen traveled toward Jerusalem, I'm sure many beggars and kings wondered what she thought she was going to accomplish by giving such a huge gift to a man who was already filthy rich. But she wasn't giving the money to help Solomon. She gave that gift to help herself. She used it to gain entry and to partake of Solomon's wisdom, favor, and anointing—and she ended up leaving Jerusalem with all of the bounty Solomon gave her. So on her return journey, she still had tremendous wealth to use to aid beggars and farmers, but she also had wisdom and anointing she could use to build her entire nation. Benevolent giving would have been a short-term solution, but using wisdom and anointing to lift the kingdom out of need was a long-term solution.

It isn't wrong to give to people in need. As a matter of fact, Scripture says that if you see your brother in need and don't help, then the love of God doesn't dwell in you (1 John 3:17). So we are definitely supposed to give when we see people in need, but that isn't the only reason to give. Sometimes, like the Queen of Sheba did, you should give because you need what a church or minister can give to you. We tell our students at Charis Bible College to "sow where you want to go." In other words, if you feel called into missionary work, then find people who are doing good work in that field and support them. By partnering with them, you begin to draw on the anointing and experience they have. It will come to you and help you fulfill your own calling.

It's kind of like finding someone who has reached a destination you want to travel to, and latching on to them to help you get there. You find someone who has gone further than you have gone, and you sow into their life to help get yourself to the same place; that's what the Queen of Sheba did. She found a person who had more favor, more wisdom, and greater wealth, and she used a gift to gain access to him in order to glean more wisdom, wealth, and favor for herself.

It's important to recognize that when you partner with a ministry and give deliberately, you can partake of the blessing that is on that ministry. Not giving just to get, but giving to help bring you where you want to go. When you do that, it starts a supernatural flow of God's finances toward you so that you are able to both meet your own needs and also abound unto every good work (2 Corinthians 9:8).

God won't let you out give Him. God always blesses you back when you show faith in Him by giving of your substance. You will never be more faithful to God than He is to you. I'm not saying that partnering with a ministry is about giving just to get; that's why I spent so much time earlier talking about your heart motives being more important than the gift itself. But when your heart is right, partnering with a ministry to help it get the Gospel out is going to open up doors for you and cause you to prosper.

Giving is a powerful part of tapping into God's prosperity. Several different things help determine the harvest you get from your giving—like the attitude you give with, where you give, and trusting God as your source—so there isn't a formula. But you can't really prosper in God's economy until you start sowing into His kingdom. I recommend you do it regularly, by tithing and giving from the firstfruits of your income; that way you won't spend your money before you can give and end up missing out on God's supernatural supply. As you become a deliberate, on-purpose giver—and you do it motivated by love—it will start a flow of God's blessings into your life that will cause you to prosper like never before.

Chapter 10

In God We Trust

When it comes to prosperity, the first thing a lot of people teach about is giving. They put the greatest emphasis on "Give, and it shall be given unto you" (Luke 6:38). Giving is one of the last things I discuss when I teach on finances because I think the heart attitude you have toward money and the motive you give with are more important. Now I want to tie it all together and show how giving with the right attitude, and in the full knowledge that God is your source, will really prosper you.

A well-known scripture tells us to trust in the Lord with all our hearts and lean not on our own understanding. It's a powerful verse, and we hear it used a lot. In context, it is part of a passage that describes how one of the ways we trust in the Lord and lean not on our own understanding is by giving.

> *Trust in the LORD with all thine heart; and lean not unto thine own understanding. In all thy ways acknowledge him, and he shall direct thy paths. Be not wise in thine own eyes: fear the LORD, and depart from evil. It shall be health to thy navel, and marrow to thy bones. Honour the LORD with*

thy substance, and with the firstfruits of all thine increase:
So shall thy barns be filled with plenty, and thy presses shall
burst out with new wine.

Proverbs 3:5–10

People often talk about these verses in the sense of trusting in the Lord, but they overlook the fact that it says to honor the Lord with the firstfruits of our income. Folks will pray all day long for God to direct their paths, but they don't see how giving is connected. Most individuals who are seeking God's guidance regularly would say they trust in God, but not all of them are giving regularly. Well, if you aren't giving, then you aren't acknowledging and trusting the Lord in all of your ways. And according to this passage, you aren't honoring God.

Finances are an important part of our lives and an important part of our relationship with God. Many people work forty or more hours a week, which means we spend more time at making a living than anything else we do, and God wants to be involved in all of our ways. If you spend the majority of your time working a job yet you aren't trusting God with your finances, then you are only trusting God with a small portion of your life. But God wants us to trust Him fully and to let Him into every area of our lives.

God doesn't want you plowing through the week, doing your own thing, and then devoting Sunday to church and Bible study. Even if you spend thirty minutes every morning praying and studying the Word, but then march into your day without giving God hardly another thought, you aren't letting God into much of your life. God wants to be a part of everything you do.

You don't have to sit around praying or studying the Bible all day to be spending time with God. Even preachers have other things to do besides study the Bible. We all have lots of things vying for our attention, but we can still keep our minds focused on God. It doesn't matter what your situation is, you can trust God with all of your heart even when you're on the job. You might have a boss and quotas to meet, but ultimately God is the One who promotes you: "Promotion cometh neither from the east, nor from the west, nor from the south. But God is the judge: he putteth down one, and setteth up another" (Psalm 75:6–7).

Taking ten percent of what you make and giving it away makes no sense to the natural mind—and that is exactly why God asks us to do it!

In other words, God is the source of everything. We should be looking to God as the source of our prosperity and promotion. Even if you punch a clock and work for someone else, God should be your source. If you don't already have that mindset, once you get it, then economic hard times won't bother you. Instead of being fearful about your job security, you'll trust in the Lord—and even if you do lose your job, you'll trust God for something better. Knowing that God is your source gives you a peace and stability in life that a lot of people don't have.

So, how do you make God your source when you are spending most of your time working and fulfilling other responsibilities? It's simple: the Lord tells us to give the firstfruits of all our increase. The way you act on your faith and make God your source is by giving—by tithing and making offerings—because if you didn't believe God was going to bless you back, it would be crazy to give away your livelihood.

Unless you factor faith in God into the equation, it makes no sense that giving would lead to prosperity. Taking ten percent of what you make and giving it away seems foolish to the natural mind—and that is exactly why God asks us to do it! God isn't broke. He doesn't need our ten percent. Giving is a way of demonstrating that we are in God's economy, not the world's.

As I've said, God could have set it up differently. He could have made every minister of the Gospel independently wealthy, but He didn't do that because giving is really about our needs—not keeping the church doors open. Even if I had billions and billions of dollars in a bank somewhere, I would still minister on finances in the exact same way. I would still take up offerings and teach about the need for Christians to give. Not because God needs our money, but because we need to trust God! The Lord set up this system of tithes and offerings for our benefit, not His.

Some time ago, I was asked to hold a meeting at the church of a Charis Bible College graduate who was pastor of a church way up in the mountains. I'm not sure, but I think there were around thirty or fifty people in the church. He was concerned that his church wasn't big enough to have me as a guest speaker, so he invited a few other local churches too. Altogether, there were probably around one hundred people who attended the meeting. Still, they were very concerned about finances and thinking they wouldn't be able to give me a good enough offering.

I started the very first meeting by telling them that I wasn't a poor preacher who was there to beg for money. I told them, "I got here on my own, and I'll leave on my own. I don't need you to give." When I said that, you could see the disappointment on the pastor's face. I guess he thought no one was going to give because I had given them an excuse not to. I went on to teach some of the same things I've written in this book. I told them they needed to give to plant a seed for themselves, not because I needed the money. I said that giving is about recognizing God as our source and trusting in Him.

The week after I left, the pastor called me to say that his church had never given so much as they gave during my meetings. He realized that he had been using the wrong motivation to get his people to give. He had been asking for money apologetically, not understanding what an important part giving plays in trusting God. He told me how he had gotten up in front of his church the following Sunday and repented in front of his congregation for not being strong enough in teaching finances. When he was done talking, his congregation came to the front to hug him and they just started throwing money on the platform. He said they paid off their entire church indebtedness in that one service—something like ten or fifteen thousand dollars.

It all started from recognizing that tithing and giving has nothing to do with God needing our money. God just wants us to trust Him, instead of looking to ourselves or our employer as our source. It's difficult for the natural mind to take a portion of what we have and give it away. It seems like we are moving away from our goals by tithing, and we would be if God hadn't promised to give back to us abundantly. Giving is about trusting God in this area that consumes more of our time and energy than any other part of our lives. We get there by taking a portion of what God gives us and giving it back to Him.

A scripture we've been looking at about trusting God with our giving says, "Honour the Lord with thy substance, and with the firstfruits of all thine increase" (Proverbs 3:9). *Firstfruits* means the very first thing we do—not after we take care of our car payment, food, and entertainment. The Lord is saying that the first thing we should do any time we get money is set aside some to give. I'm not condemning anyone for not giving. What I'm trying to do is remove the deception that has caused a lot of Christians to compartmentalize their lives and separate serving the Lord from giving.

Some believers are trying to trust God, but they aren't giving because they don't see how they can squeeze it out of their budget. This is the reason the Lord didn't tell you to give a specific amount. God put a percentage on giving because everyone can give ten percent, whether you have a million dollars or a dime.

When you honor God by giving with the firstfruits of your increase, then the Lord turns around and says, "So shall thy barns be filled with plenty, and thy presses shall burst out with new wine" (v. 10). The way we would say that today is, "I'm going to fill up your checking account, and your savings account is going to burst." Giving is how you wind up with a huge savings—not by hoarding. When you take a portion of what you have and trust God with it, then it becomes a seed that yields greater increase in the future.

You can get strength and sustenance by eating seeds, but you also need enough wisdom to set aside a portion of those seeds for planting. You can't eat those seeds, even when you're hungry, because eating all of your seed now means starving tomorrow. Planting seed ensures that you have a crop in the future to feed your family and provide for your needs.

Most people are short-term thinkers. They don't see the wisdom in giving because the natural mind can't understand the things of the spirit. (See 1 Corinthians 2:14.) A lot of folks are struggling financially, and their natural minds don't see how they can spare any of their income toward giving. The mind sees that there isn't enough and concludes that we need to keep everything, but the Word of God says honor the Lord with the firstfruits of our substance and our bank accounts will burst forth with finances.

> *Giving is really about trusting God and acting on your faith.*

God says the way to abundance is by giving—or you could say that it's by trusting God because giving boils down to trust. Remember, the Lord asks us to give so that we will learn to rely on Him. Ironically, the people who are most reluctant to give and are most convinced that they need all of their money are the people who need to trust God the most. Faith without works is dead (James 2:26). You have to act on your faith. Don't take this the wrong way, but if you aren't tithing, then you aren't trusting God. *Giving* is a step of faith that turns your focus to God and moves you into position to receive from Him.

As I've said before, God isn't mad at you if you aren't tithing. He's not going to come and get you. But if you aren't giving, then you aren't really trusting God. It's a Scriptural principle that if you want to prosper through God, then you are going to have to learn to give.

Look at this verse from Proverbs: "There is that scattereth, and yet increaseth; and there is that withholdeth more than is meet, but it tendeth to poverty" (Proverbs 11:24). To the natural mind, this doesn't make any sense. How can scattering lead to prosperity, and withholding lead to poverty? Yet that is how God's economy works. You can't understand it with your natural mind. The world prospers by hoarding, but God reveals that the way to supernatural prosperity is through giving. When you don't tithe or give because you think you need everything, you are "withholding more than is meet," and it leads to poverty. If you want to prosper, take a step of faith, and start giving.

The longer you have been following the thinking of this world, the less sense any of this is going to make. But according to the promises of Scripture, God gives back to you when you give in faith. It's when you scatter that your barns are filled with plenty and your presses burst forth with new wine. Giving is your way to prosperity! You can't operate in financial prosperity through God's system without trusting God with your finances and being a faithful giver.

The next verse in Proverbs 11 says, "The liberal soul shall be made fat: and he that watereth shall be watered also himself" (v. 25). This is stating the same principle we discussed earlier about God giving seed to sowers. God gives money to people who are going to sow into His kingdom, not to people who are just going to keep it all. "The liberal soul shall be made fat," is another way of saying that when you are a giver, you will have more money than you need. You'll have riches in reserve. God will bless you and multiply you.

This also shows that you reap what you sow (Galatians 6:7). If you give a little, you get a little—but when you give liberally, you get liberally. When you sow a lot, you reap a lot. Nearly everyone wants to reap a lot, but they try sowing as little as possible; it doesn't work that way. You can't give by the teaspoon and expect to receive by the truckload. If you want to receive by the truckload, then you have to give by the truckload.

Fortunately, God's kingdom is set up on percentages. You don't have to literally give huge amounts of money. God looks at your giving in proportion to how much you have. For instance, Jesus said that the widow who dropped two mites in the offering gave more than all of the rich men who gave to the Temple treasury. The rich men gave out of their abundance, but the widow woman gave all that she had (Luke 21:1–4; Mark 12:41–44). So it's not just about how much you give or what percentage of your income it is, it's also about how much money you have leftover after giving.

The pastor friend I mentioned earlier who bought a number of cars for me is a prosperous man, and he lives like it. He lives in an expensive house, has nice clothes, and his "weakness" is nice cars. I was at his house once when a truck drove up and unloaded a brand-new red Corvette. It was hot. It had two ignition keys. If you really wanted to go fast, you started the second ignition. The insurance on that vehicle was $1,000 per month.

Many people criticize him for his lifestyle. They only look at what he has and not what he gives. But you should never criticize a person's harvest until you see how much seed they have planted.

I was at his house another time when he gave me $20,000 for preaching one service at his church. A missionary friend was at church that morning and he gave him $10,000. Another minister friend was also there and he gave him a brand-new Cadillac that same morning. Altogether, my friend gave away over $70,000 in one day. He probably averaged giving away $40,000 per month. So, his house only cost about sixteen months of his giving. Would you want to live in a house that equaled sixteen months of your giving? You might be living in a tent.

My pastor friend's Corvette was a gift with the insurance included. What should he have done—turn a free car with prepaid insurance down and go buy something that cost him money just so he could look poor and be more humble? That's not humility. That's stupidity.

God doesn't care what you drive or what kind of house you live in. It's all relative to your giving. This man gave a lot and he reaped a lot. You can't out give God. When he took care of others, God took care of him.

The widow who gave two mites in the Temple offering gave the equivalent of maybe half a penny, but she gave the most because she gave her entire livelihood—that's what God calls a liberal giver. If all you have is one dollar and you give it away, then that is a huge gift.

But don't go giving all of your money away! God wants you to take care of your family. He wants you to eat and provide for your needs. He doesn't want you to be broke and living under a bridge. The point here is just that God wants you to trust Him. It's easy for a wealthy person to throw $1,000 in the offering plate; whereas a person who is barely getting by but still tithes with joy is showing trust in God. Giving liberally isn't about the cash value of your gift.

You can be so wealthy that ten percent of your income won't even put a dent in your spending. In that case, tithing might not be enough to build trust in God as your source. If you have come to a level of prosperity where giving ten percent is no skin off your teeth, then you should increase your giving to where you still need to trust God to multiply your finances. Give to where you are relying on God to come through for you financially. It's all about trust.

The passage in Proverbs goes on to say, "He that trusteth in his riches shall fall: but the righteous shall flourish as a branch" (Proverbs 11:28). This is the same thing Jesus was trying to teach the rich young man we looked at earlier. He told that man to sell everything he owned and give the proceeds to the poor. The young ruler fell at Jesus' feet and asked what he needed to do in order to be saved, but Jesus knew that the man wasn't really trusting in Him. The man's trust was in his money. By asking the man to sell everything, Jesus was telling him to start looking to God as his source. It's the same thing the Lord is telling us when He asks us to tithe. He's telling us to stop trusting money and to put our trust in Him. When our trust is in God, we prosper—we flourish as a branch.

I don't see any exception to this. You can try to explain it any way you want, but if you aren't honoring the Lord with your firstfruits, the bottom line is that you don't trust God. Fear that God won't come through for you is what is keeping you from giving, and that fear is actually releasing poverty into your life. If that's the case, then all you have to do is start taking steps of faith by giving. Honoring the Lord with your firstfruits will release the power and anointing of God in your life, and you will begin to prosper. It's simple.

Many people are praying and asking God to bless them financially yet they are afraid to follow His instructions about tithing. Giving is an absolutely integral part of godly prosperity, but remember that your motive is more important than the gift. Don't try to give just so you can get—it won't work. Whatever you do, do it heartily as unto the Lord, and God will cause it to prosper (Colossians 3:23–24).

Giving keeps your heart focused on the Lord. Trusting in God as your source lets Him into your finances. You won't just spend a little devotional time in the morning and then shut God out and go through the rest of the day in your own ability. God doesn't want you to divide your life into a "spiritual" part that prays and a carnal part that works and takes care of day-to-day responsibilities.

One of the ways we can learn to put God first is by taking a portion of what He gives us and giving it back to Him. Your heart will be where your treasure is (Matthew 6:21). Consistently investing money in the kingdom will keep you single-minded on God. Even though you have to work a job, you will know that God is your source.

Paul's letter to the Galatians says, "Be not deceived; God is not mocked: for whatsoever a man soweth, that shall he also reap" (Galatians 6:7). The *Amplified Bible* says, "For whatever a man sows, that *and* that only is what he will reap." You don't reap something you haven't sown; you aren't going to reap potatoes if you sow carrots. If you want love, you have to sow love. If you want acceptance, then sow acceptance. And if you want finances, you are going to have to sow finances. To reap a harvest of prosperity, you have to sow resources by giving. A scripture we saw earlier says,

> *Give, and it shall be given unto you; good measure, pressed down, and shaken together, and running over, shall men give into your bosom. For with the same measure that ye mete withal it shall be measured to you again.*

Luke 6:38

The way you give is how you receive. Are you giving off the top? Is tithing the first thing you do when you get income? If you're slow to give, then you're going to be slow to receive. Some people wait until the last possible moment, and then they give grudgingly or of necessity. They don't really want to give, but they feel like they have to. Then they wonder why their needs aren't supplied right away. The reason is this law: you not only reap *what* you sow, you reap the *way* you sow.

You not only reap what you sow, you reap the way you sow.

I know I've already made these points, but I keep coming back to them from different scriptures because I'm hoping that the weight of all this evidence will convince you. I'm hoping you'll get a revelation that if you want to prosper in God's system, then you have to start giving—and you can't just grudgingly give a little bit if you want to get a lot in return. You have to give a lot,[16] you have to do it cheerfully, and you have to give from the firstfruits. If you do those things over a prolonged period of time, then you can start to see a crop come in.

Sadly, the majority of Christians do not tithe and give offerings. Pastors have been saying for a long time that around 20 percent of the people give 80–100 percent of the church's finances. From talking to pastors and reading reports on giving, I'd have to say I believe it. So a lot of believers don't understand this cardinal law that if you want to prosper through God's financial system, then you have to be a giver.

I think the main reason people don't give is because of fear—fear that they won't have enough to take care of their families, or fear that God won't come through for them. I hope I have presented enough Scripture to counter that fear and unbelief, and to assure you that once you start giving and trusting God with your finances, He will make you prosper!

When the apostle Paul had something important to tell the believers, he would say, "I *beseech* ye brethren." It's like saying, "I implore you." Well, I'm imploring you to start trusting God with your finances; it's for your own good. The whole reason God told us to give is to let Him into our finances.

If you have money, then you can give. It doesn't matter how much you have. Trust what God's Word says and begin to give from

---

[16] Remember, giving a lot is in proportion to what you have. If you only have a dollar to give, that is a huge gift.

your firstfruits. Don't hold back for fear that you won't have enough.

God will provide. He wants to bless you financially, but you have to plant seed. You need to take a step of faith. So start giving, and watch for God's supernatural flow to increase your finances and cause you to prosper in every area of your life.

Receive Jesus as Your Savior

Choosing to receive Jesus Christ as your Lord and Savior is the most important decision you'll ever make!

God's Word promises, "That if thou shalt confess with thy mouth the Lord Jesus, and shalt believe in thine heart that God hath raised him from the dead, thou shalt be saved. For with the heart man believeth unto righteousness; and with the mouth confession is made unto salvation" (Romans 10:9–10). "For whosoever shall call upon the name of the Lord shall be saved" (Romans 10:13).

By His grace, God has already done everything to provide salvation. Your part is simply to believe and receive.

Pray out loud: Jesus, I confess that You are my Lord and Savior. I believe in my heart that God raised You from the dead. By faith in Your Word, I receive salvation now. Thank You for saving me.

The very moment you commit your life to Jesus Christ, the truth of His Word instantly comes to pass in your spirit. Now that you're born again, there's a brand-new you.

Receive the Holy Spirit

As His child, your loving heavenly Father wants to give you the supernatural power you need to live this new life.

For every one that asketh receiveth; and he that seeketh findeth; and to him that knocketh it shall be opened...how much more shall your heavenly Father give the Holy Spirit to them that ask him?

Luke 11:10 and 13

All you have to do is ask, believe, and receive!

Pray: Father, I recognize my need for Your power to live this new life. Please fill me with Your Holy Spirit. By faith, I receive it right now. Thank You for baptizing me. Holy Spirit, You are welcome in my life.

Congratulations—now you're filled with God's supernatural power.

Some syllables from a language you don't recognize will rise up from your heart to your mouth (1 Corinthians 14:14). As you speak them out loud by faith, you're releasing God's power from within and building yourself up in the spirit (1 Corinthians 14:4). You can do this whenever and wherever you like.

It doesn't really matter whether you felt anything or not when you prayed to receive the Lord and His Spirit. If you believed in your heart that you received, then God's Word promises you did. "Therefore I say unto you, What things soever ye desire, when ye pray, believe that ye receive them, and ye shall have them" (Mark 11:24). God always honors His Word—believe it!

Please contact me and let me know that you've prayed to receive Jesus as your Savior or be filled with the Holy Spirit. I would like to rejoice with you and help you understand more fully what has taken place in your life. I'll send you a free gift that will help you understand and grow in your new relationship with the Lord. "Welcome to your new life!"

About the Author

ANDREW WOMMACK'S life was forever changed the moment he encountered the supernatural love of God on March 23, 1968. As a renowned Bible teacher and author, Andrew has made it his mission to change the way the world sees God.

Andrew's vision is to go as far and deep with the Gospel as possible. His message goes far through the *Gospel Truth* television program, which is available to nearly half the world's population. The message goes deep through discipleship at Charis Bible College, headquartered in Woodland Park, Colorado. Founded in 1994, Charis has campuses across the United States and around the globe.

Andrew also has an extensive library of teaching materials in print, audio, and video—most of which can be accessed for free from his website: **awmi.net**.

Contact Us

We'd love to hear from you!
Reach out to us at any of our offices near you.

AWM Offices

Andrew Wommack Ministries USA
Headquarters—Woodland Park, CO
Website: awmi.net
Email: info@awmi.net

Andrew Wommack Ministries Australia
Website: awmaust.net.au
Email: info@awmaust.net.au

Andrew Wommack Ministries Canada
Website: awmc.ca
Email: info@awmc.ca

Andrew Wommack Ministries France
Website: awmi.fr
Email: info@awmi.fr

Andrew Wommack Ministries Germany
Website: andrewwommack.de
Email: info@andrewwommack.de

Andrew Wommack Ministries Hong Kong
Website: awmi.hk
Email: info@awmi.hk

Andrew Wommack Ministries Hungary
Website: awme.hu
Email: hungary@awme.net

Andrew Wommack Ministries Indonesia
Website: awmindonesia.net
Email: awmindonesia@gmail.com

Andrew Wommack Ministries India
Website: awmindia.net
Email: info@awmindia.net

Andrew Wommack Ministries Italy
Website: awme.it
Email: info@awme.it

Andrew Wommack Ministries Lithuania
Website: awmi.lt
Email: charis@charis.lt

Andrew Wommack Ministries Netherlands
Website: andrewwommack.nl
Email: info.nl@awmcharis.com

Andrew Wommack Ministries Poland
Website: awmpolska.com
Email: awmpolska@zyciesozo.com

Andrew Wommack Ministries Russia
Website: cbtcrussia.ru
Email: info@cbtcrussia.ru

Andrew Wommack Ministries South Africa
Website: awmsa.net
Email: enquiries@awmsa.net

Andrew Wommack Ministries Uganda
Website: awmuganda.net
Email: awm.uga@awmcharis.com

Andrew Wommack Ministries United Kingdom
Website: awme.net
Email: enquiries@awme.net

Andrew Wommack Ministries Zimbabwe
Website: awmzim.net
Email: enquiries@awmzim.net

For a more comprehensive list of all of
our offices, visit **awmi.net/contact-us**.

Connect with us on social media

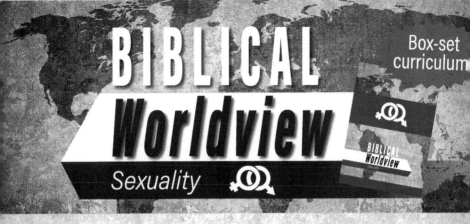

BIBLICAL Worldview
Sexuality

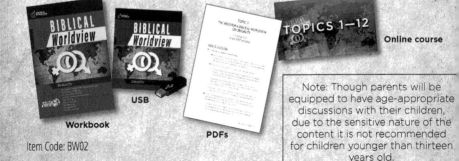

Andrew's
LIVING COMMENTARY BIBLE SOFTWARE

Andrew Wommack's *Living Commentary* Bible study software is a user-friendly, downloadable program. It's like reading the Bible with Andrew at your side, sharing his revelation with you verse by verse.

Main features:

- Access to Windows, Mac, and web versions
- Andrew Wommack's notes on over 25,000 Scriptures and counting
- 11 Bible versions, 5 commentaries, 3 concordances, and 2 dictionaries
- Maps and charts
- User notes
- Enhanced text selection and copying
- Commentaries and charts
- Scripture-reveal and note-reveal functionalities
- "Living" (i.e., constantly updated)
- Quick navigation
- Robust search capabilities
- Automatic software updates
- Mobile phone and tablet support for web version
- Screen reader support for visually impaired users (Windows version)
- Bonus material

Whether you're new to studying the Bible or a seasoned Bible scholar, you'll gain a deeper revelation of the Word from a grace-and-faith perspective.

Purchase Andrew's *Living Commentary* today at **awmi.net/living**, and grow in the Word with Andrew.

Item code: 8350